Pacific Coast Fish

by Ron Russo
illustrated by Ann Caudle

a guide to marine fish of the Pacific coast of North America

How to use this book:

If you have a fish you want to identify, see pages 12 - 15.

If you want to know about the biology of:

- · fish in general, pages 1 - 11
- · sharks, p. 16
- · salmon, p. 41
- · rockfish, p. 53
- · surfperch, p. 69
- · tunas, p. 91
- · flatfish, p. 96

If you've found a brittle or leathery-brown case, see p. 19.

If you've found a tooth, see p. 20.

This book includes some of the common marine fish you're likely to encounter while fishing or diving along this coast. Many other species are known to occur here.

Ron Russo is chief naturalist for the East Bay Regional Park District, Oakland, California. He received the 1989 Fellow Award of the National Association for Interpretation.

Ann Caudle teaches Science Illustration at the University of California, Santa Cruz.

©1990 Nature Study Guild   Cover by Erica Watts.

The Biology of Fish

In the course of evolution, fish have exploited nearly every aquatic habitat. From freezing Arctic waters to the hot pools of Death Valley, fish have adapted to diverse conditions. Today, over 21,000 species inhabit the seas, lakes, rivers, ponds and the tiniest of streams on earth. But survival in polluted or contaminated waters is as difficult for fish as it is for other life forms.

Common Features

There are three main groups of fish: jawless fish (hagfish, lampreys), cartilaginous fish (sharks, rays), and bony fish (salmon, perch). The fish in each group vary in size, shape, color, and ecological roles. But all fish tend to share some common features that aid their survival.

Skin, Scales and Slime

Skin is an important organ. It protects and encloses a fish's body, and regulates oxygen exchange, excretion and water pressure. It has sense organs, nerves, and blood vessels, as well as pigment-bearing cells called chromatophores. The skin is protected by slime, secreted by its mucous-producing cells and, in many species, by hard overlapping scales.

You can often tell a fish's age by counting the microscopic growth rings in its scales. Evidence of disease, injury, starvation, pollution and other unfavorable conditions in a fish's life can also be found as a microscopic record in fish scales.

Fins

Fins are supported by soft cartilage or by hard, bony spines or rays. They're used as propellers, rudders, stabilizers, brakes, and hydroplanes, or as ingenious anti-roll devices to maintain proper orientation. Some fish use their fins as limbs to "walk" along the bottom. Rockfishes and surfperches often use fins to signal aggression or interest in mating. Some sharks use pectoral fins to warn of imminent attack.

Vision

In most bony fish, the position of eyes allows a field of view extending nearly 360 degrees, letting them see prey and predators. Most fish are considered farsighted. Fish living in dark, deep, or murky waters tend to have larger eyes than ones in light, shallow, or clear waters. Many bony fish detect color.

Hearing and Sound

Fish have three structures sensitive to sound. High frequency sound is picked up by the inner ear and by the swimbladder. Low frequencies are detected by the lateral-line system, a well defined canal that runs along mid-body and branches over the head and face. Within these canals are sensitive hair cells that are bent by low-frequency vibrations.

Some species make sound by: grinding teeth in the back of the mouth; moving two bones in the pectoral girdle; or by vibrating the walls of the swimbladder with special muscles. Such sound functions in courtship, spawning, defense, migration. It enables schooling fish to warn each other of danger.

Breathing

Oxygen is absorbed and carbon dioxide is released as water passes over the intricate network of capillaries in a fish's gills. Fish have a coughing or sneezing reflex to eject foreign matter that might otherwise clog the gills and cause suffocation. Some fish can absorb oxygen by gulping air.

Color

Pigments are housed in specialized skin cells called chromatophores. Each chromatophore has a specific color. Nerves connected to chromatophores control intensity of color by concentrating or dispersing the pigment. In this way, fish can change color to match their surroundings, to defend territory or advertize readiness for mating.

The intensity of some color is influenced by secretions from the pituitary gland. Other apparent color is produced not by pigment, but by refraction of light reflected back to the viewer. Iridescent greens, blues and browns are produced this way. Silver color is due to the reflection of light off crystalline guanine, a metabolic waste product. Black pigments are also waste products.

Many fish have dark backs and light bellies. This pattern, called counter shading, compensates for the sunlight on the back and the shadow on the belly so that the fish are less noticeable viewed from the side. Counter-shaded fish blend with the lighter background of the surface when viewed from below, and with the dark background of the bottom when viewed from above.

Swimbladder

There is a gas filled swimbladder between the stomach and the spine of most bony fish. It controls buoyancy. As a fish rises, dis-solved gas leaves the blood, expands the bladder, increasing buoyancy. When the fish sinks, increased pressure forces bladder gas back into the blood, decreasing buoyancy. The buoyancy stabilizes as the fish holds to a given depth. Bony fish without swim bladders (flatfish and sculpins) habitually rest on the bottom. Non-bony sharks and rays also lack swimbladders.

Salt Balance

All fish have dissolved salts essential to survival in their flesh and blood. These salts are maintained at specific levels of concentration. The levels often differ from the concentrations in the surrounding water. Water tends to move from an area of low salt concentration to an area of higher concentration. It can either leave or enter the fish's body through the membranes covering its gills, mouth and pharynx. This process can alter the salt concentrations, making the fish either too salty, or not salty enough. Fish have adapted to this problem in several ways. The bodies of freshwater fish have higher salt concentrations than the surrounding water. They are, then, in danger of flooding their cells. To compensate, they produce high volumes of urine.

In marine bony fish, the reverse is true. They are less salty than sea water and in constant danger of dehydration. To compensate, marine fish drink 10-40% of their body weight daily, excreting excess salts through special cells in their gills, and producing very little urine.

Sharks and rays, on the other hand, have slightly higher salt concentrations than the sea. They prevent dilution of the required salt level by keeping high levels of urea in their blood, which equalizes the internal and external environments.

When marine fish enter fresh water, they slowly reverse their normal habits to maintain the proper balance of salts.

Schooling

Anchovy, herring, mackerel, smelt, tuna, some rockfish, and other species often form groups, or schools, of up to thousands of like-sized fish. Simple aggregations of fish disperse when startled, but schools draw together, tightening up their formation when startled.

To some predators, a school may appear as a single giant organism. Fish attacking a school may also be confused and deterred by the difficulty of focusing on any given individual within the school, as its members dart and turn in near-perfect unison. The many sets of eyes in a school help schooling fish to detect and warn each other of danger, and make foraging more efficient. But it's no guarantee of survival. Barracuda, tuna, thresher sharks and some other predators are adept at feeding on schooling fish. Finally, schooling makes it easier to find a mate and successfully spawn.

Parasites

No fish is totally free of parasites. Various small crustaceans called copepods penetrate the protective slime to feed between the scales of fish on their body juices. The bodies and fin edges of sharks often bear such external parasites. A marine leech, *Branchellion lobata* regularly attaches itself to the lining of the mouth, the claspers, the surface of the eyes, and the soft tissues at the free edges of fins in a variety of sharks. The gill louse, *Lironeca vulgaris* attaches itself to the gills of both bony and cartilaginous fish. It feeds on the hormones and nutrients in the blood. Fish are not totally at the mercy of external parasites. They routinely scrape against rocks or sand to dislodge their hitchhikers. Some fish use the cleaning services of other fish or shrimps who specialize in removing parasites.

Internal parasites: tapeworms, roundworms, threadworms and flatworms are common in intestines, hearts, livers, muscles and blood. Normally, these do not imperil the life of the host fish. **CAUTION: Be sure to cook fish thoroughly before consumption**.

Locations in Text

Locations in parentheses indicate instances where the behavior of a species at the given locality is reported in scientific literature. The behavior in question takes place elsewhere within the range of the species, but we cite only the location where it has been reliably observed.

Typical Body Parts of Cartilaginous Fish

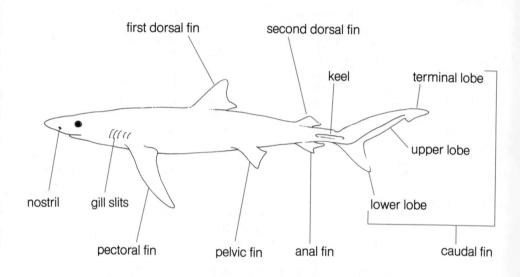

(Fish illustrated is blue shark.)

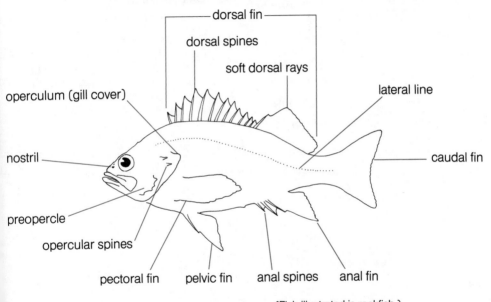

(Fish illustrated is rockfish.)

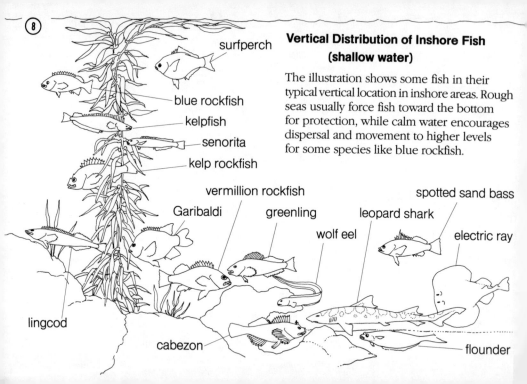

⑧

surfperch

blue rockfish

kelpfish

senorita

kelp rockfish

**Vertical Distribution of Inshore Fish
(shallow water)**

The illustration shows some fish in their typical vertical location in inshore areas. Rough seas usually force fish toward the bottom for protection, while calm water encourages dispersal and movement to higher levels for some species like blue rockfish.

vermillion rockfish

spotted sand bass

Garibaldi

greenling

leopard shark

electric ray

wolf eel

lingcod

cabezon

flounder

Vertical Distribution of Offshore Fish
(deep water)

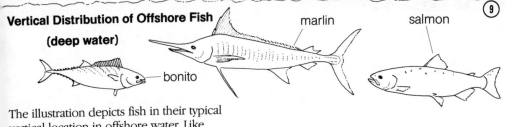

bonito

marlin

salmon

The illustration depicts fish in their typical vertical location in offshore water. Like all mobile creatures, they may visit other levels and areas. Tomcod, for instance, frequent both bottom and surface at different times. Blue sharks typically spend their days offshore in deep water, but at night, particularly near islands, they swim into shallow water well above the 500 foot level, sometimes even to the surface. On the other hand, marlin, bonito, and salmon usually feed near the surface.

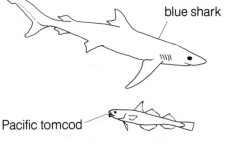

blue shark

Pacific tomcod

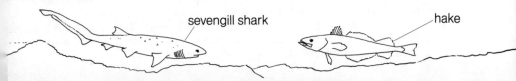

sevengill shark

hake

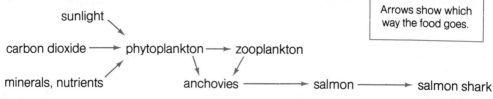

Arrows show which way the food goes.

Pacific coast waters have upwelling currents which bring up a mix of minerals and organic compounds representing the remains of countless creatures that die and settle in deep water. The food chain illustrated above begins when phytoplankton, minute drifting plants, use these minerals and nutrients, plus carbon dioxide, and the energy in sunlight, to produce oxygen and their own food. The plants multiply and become food for the zooplankton: tiny drifting animals like copepods, and the larvae of crabs, shrimp, barnacles, etc. Plankton are strained from the water by anchovies, who in turn are eaten by salmon who are eaten by salmon sharks.

In the above food chain, each link represents a transfer of energy, from prey to predator. The predator burns up some of this energy for its own metabolism, and uses the rest to grow larger and, if lucky, to reproduce.

Energy accumulates in the larger fish as they eat the smaller ones. An anchovy consumes countless minute planktonic creatures in its life. In turn it takes hundreds of anchovies to produce a 20 pound salmon, and many salmon to produce a full-grown salmon shark. The salmon shark is the top predator in its food chain just as white sharks, sperm whales, and humans are in theirs.

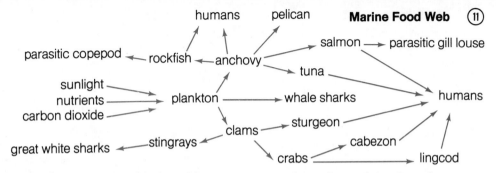

The above food web outlines a few of the interactions among marine organisms. Every element in the web depends directly or indirectly on phytoplankton. These relationships become vastly more complex than a simple food chain.

A complete food web would include all relationships between species: the predators and parasites, the many ways species use each other for shelter, transportation, and protection, the production and recycling of carbon dioxide, oxygen, and metabolic wastes, the settling and recycling of organic material from ocean depths…and more. Many of these relationships have been identified, but most of them remain to be discovered.

However, biologists do know enough to understand that reckless tampering with this complex web through reduction or extermination of species or by pollution of their environment, endangers all life including our own.

Identification Guide

Fish on the next four pages are arranged by shape (but they are not drawn precisely to scale). See page indicated for more detail.

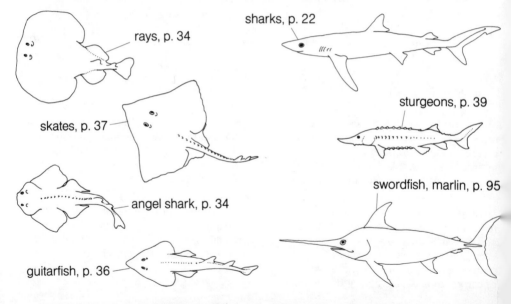

rays, p. 34

sharks, p. 22

skates, p. 37

sturgeons, p. 39

angel shark, p. 34

swordfish, marlin, p. 95

guitarfish, p. 36

sheepshead, p. 88

opaleye, p. 90

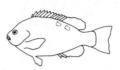

Garibaldi, p. 85

surfperches, p. 70

flatfish, flounder, p. 104

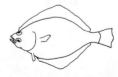

blacksmith, p. 86

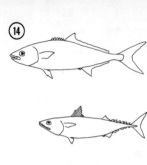

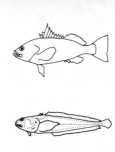 sand bass,
kelp bass, p. 81

rockfish, p. 53-68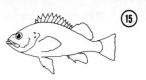

 midshipman, p. 45

senorita, p. 88

 lizardfish, p. 45

barracuda, p. 87

 cod, p. 46
tomcod, p. 47

wolf-eel, p. 87

 smelt,
eulachon, p. 44
grunion, p. 47

monkeyface eel,
p. 89

hake, p. 46

kelpfish, p. 89

Few other creatures in the sea elicit the intense, bone-chilling response in people who swim, dive or sail that sharks do. But of over 300 known shark species, only about a dozen attack people, and usually do so only in response to provocation, or perhaps because they sense distress in the victim, or mistake a human for a sea lion. Most sharks are either too small to bother people, or they live in deep water, or they're harmless giants who feed on plankton, fish or other small creatures. They range in size from a six-inch Japanese species to the 38-foot whale shark. They occupy all the oceans. A few species swim well up into rivers and one lives in Lake Nicaragua, in Central America.

Unfortunately, the biology of most shark species is not well known because few specimens have ever been examined and observed. Our understanding is based on some species that have been studied thoroughly.

Sharks have a cartilaginous skeleton instead of bones. Their razor-sharp teeth, made of dentine, are a modified form of the scales covering their skin. Sharks lack swim bladders, so they must constantly swim or rest on the bottom. They also lack single, external gill covers. Instead, each set of gills is exposed directly to the outside through thin slits in the sides of their heads.

Just under the skin of the face and head, sharks have a network of jelly-filled canals or tubes which connect to the lateral line, and open to the outside through pores. These canals, called the Ampullae of Lorenzini, enable the shark to detect weak electrical fields at short range, and thereby find prey in total darkness or prey buried in sand. Just behind the eyes of most sharks are tiny holes called **spiracles** which are vestigial gill slits that provide oxygenated blood directly to the eyes and brain through a separate blood vessel. The position of the mouth on the underside and back from the snout allows sharks to sample or taste and smell items before biting them. Teeth are arranged in rows along the edges of each jaw, with several replacements lined up behind each tooth. A damaged or lost tooth is replaced in a matter of days with no loss of feeding efficiency to the bearer.

Although the physical features of skates and rays are quite different, the biology is generally similar to that of sharks.

Shark Reproduction

The evolutionary success of sharks, is partly due to their reproductive adaptations. They have three basic reproductive modes. Each begins with internal fertilization. Males have specialized pelvic fins shaped like stout tubes that guide sperm directly into females. Some species, including all skates, are **oviparous**, producing eggs which develop outside the parent, enclosed in leathery cases.

Most sharks are **ovoviviparous**, hatching the eggs inside the uterine canals of the female. The embryos are nourished either from large egg yolks, or by ingesting the yolks of their litter mates. Although such females produce relatively few young, the pups spend their most vulnerable period inside their parent. After completing their development, they are born relatively large, as near-perfect replicas of their parents.

The most advanced reproductive mode is in those sharks that are **viviparous**, having embryos initially dependent on yolk, but later nourished directly by the parent through a placental connection.

Because of their relatively low reproductive rate, sharks are particularly vulnerable to human ignorance, over-fishing, and poor fisheries management. Exaggerated movies have unleashed a misinformed, overzealous and maniacal shark-hunting craze in North America, the effects of which are still not fully known. The depletion of some species is of critical concern to researchers seeking, for instance, to study sharks' resistance to heart disease and cancer. But we have a greater interest in the survival of sharks. They are important predators and scavengers, and no doubt play other roles in the ocean we know little about.

swell shark
90-125mm

California skate
70-85mm

horn shark
125mm (avg.)

starry skate
71-78mm

big skate
265-305mm

(20) **Shark Teeth**

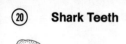 sevengill

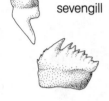

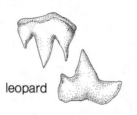 leopard

gray smoothhound

brown smoothhound

soupfin

 dogfish

 swell

horn

(Teeth are not drawn to scale.)

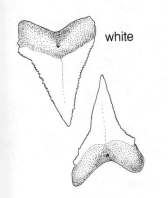
white

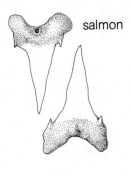
salmon

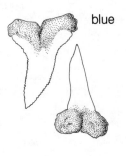
blue

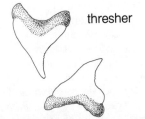
thresher

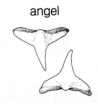
angel

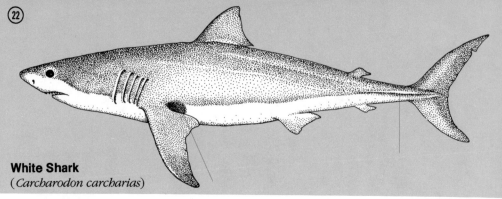

White Shark
(*Carcharodon carcharias*)

Average size 460 cm (15 ft). Some reach 640 cm (21 ft) and 4800 lbs. or larger. Color varies from lead-white to slate brown or blue above to dirty white below. Key features are torpedo-shaped snout, triangular teeth with serrated edges, and black area at base of pectoral fins. A strong swimmer, it hunts in shallow water. Specimens under three meters (9 ft) eat various fish, including rockfish, tuna, bat rays, and other sharks. Larger white sharks eat mostly marine mammals. Once attack begins, it's swift and determined, often fatal. Known to attack surfers, bathers, divers, even boats. Ovoviviparous. Newborn young are about 129 cm (51 in). Biology not well known. Found worldwide. On Pacific coast, Alaska to southern California, but most abundant between Tomales Bay and Monterey, where large colonies of its primary prey, seals and sea lions, occur.

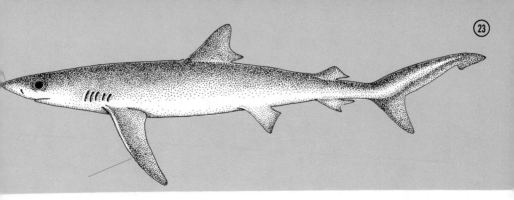

Blue Shark (*Prionace glauca*)

Average size 240 cm (8 ft), larger specimens to 380 cm (12 ft). Dark indigo blue on top, bright blue laterally. Key features are blue color, long nose, pectoral fins, and large eyes. Eats small schooling fish like anchovy, sardines, and herring. Will eat captured salmon, rockfish, squid, and wounded marine mammals. Viviparous. After 9-12 month gestation, female usually bears 25 to 50 pups, each pup about 40-51 cm (16-20 in) long.

Births of up to 135 pups are known. Young blue sharks, 76 cm (30 in) long have been seen cruising at surface near Farallon Islands in August. Adults pelagic, around islands, particularly at night. Rare near mainland. Blue shark lives in deep, clear blue water. Ranges widely along entire Pacific coast. Generally sluggish, with impressive bursts of speed and feeding frenzies. A dangerous shark.

Thresher Shark (*Alopias vulpinus*)
Individuals 300-500 cm (10-16 ft) are common. Some reach 610 cm (20 ft) and 1,000 lbs. Color varies from dark metallic brown to near black on top; underside white. Key feature is distinctive arching tail, used to stun prey. Eats mainly schooling fishes like shad, mackerel, sardines. It charges into a school, then returns to swallow wounded fish. Also eats squid. Ovoviviparous, four to six pups born per litter, 137-155 cm (54-61 in) each. Females are sexually mature at 10 feet. This is a pelagic, deep water shark, mostly caught on longline below 100 fathoms. Some caught near surface. Cosmopolitan: along our coast from British Columbia to California.

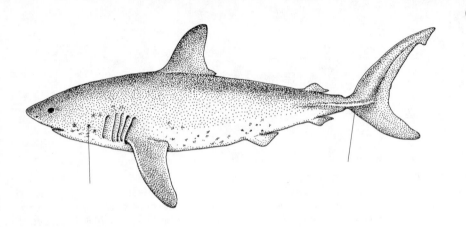

Salmon Shark (*Lamna ditropis*)

Length to 300 cm (10 ft). Dark bluish gray to blue-black above, with an abrupt change to white on the belly. This is a fast swimming pelagic species that migrates along the coast in groups of 30-40 individuals following schools of salmon. Eats salmon, tomcod, mackerel in the north and squid, lanternfish and saury in the south. The salmon shark is a major predator on salmon and destroys salmon fishing gear. Ovoviviparous. Two to four pups born per litter, 65-70 cm (26-28 in) long. From Bering Sea to San Diego.

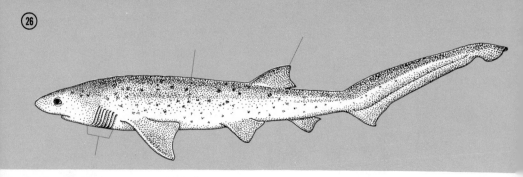

Sevengill Shark (*Notorhynchus cepedianus*)
Average size of commonly caught specimens 70-125 cm (28-49 in). Largest recorded is 296 cm (9 ft), but larger specimens probably exist. Gray to reddish brown with irregular black spots, distinct for each individual, over the sides and back. Belly white. Albinism known in this shark. Key features are broad head, large mouth, seven gill slits (instead of five), a single dorsal fin, and black spots. Eats chimaeras, mackerel, other small sharks. Feeds on long-line-caught sharks in bays, leaving only heads. Ovoviviparous. Litter size to 80 plus pups. Young about 50 cm (20 in) at birth. Adult females apparently enter bays to give birth. Immatures common in Tomales, San Francisco, Monterey Bays. Species ranges throughout Pacific and Indian oceans. Known to attack divers in large aquaria. Swims constantly; seldom rests on bottom. Has been called "Lord of the Depths." A potentially dangerous species.

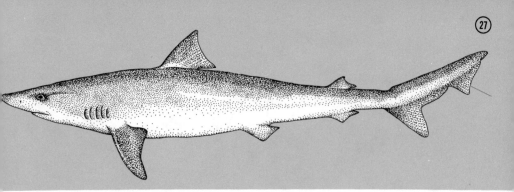

Soupfin Shark (*Galeorhinus zyopterus*)

Average size 165 cm (65 in) for males, 175 cm (69 in) for females; maximum size to 200 cm (79 in). Dark bluish gray to dark gray above; white below. Has sharp teeth. An opportunistic feeder, eating sardines, flounders, rockfish, mackerel, squid. Ovoviviparous. Gestation about 12 months; newborn pups are 35 cm (14 in). Some born in Tomales and San Francisco Bays, but major pupping grounds appear to be south of Point Conception. Males are mature at about 155 cm (61 in), females at 170 cm (67 in). There is some segregation by sex, with males abundant off northern California, and females abundant off southern California. Range is British Columbia to Baja California to Chile and Peru. Historically, this shark was an important commercial source of Vitamin A, fillets and fins for soup. Overfishing in nursery areas depleted the populations.

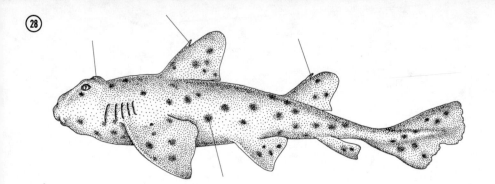

Horn Shark (*Heterodontus francisci*)
Normal adult size 90 cm (35 in) to 98 cm (39 in) or larger. Light to dark brown above, light beige on belly, with small black spots over entire body. Has sharp spine in front of each dorsal fin. Characteristic ridge over eye protects eye while shark nudges rocks in pursuit of food. Eats crabs, shrimp, clam necks, small fish. Oviparous. Lays screw-shaped, chitinous egg cases; embryos develop and hatch out in six to nine months at 15-17 cm (6-7 in). A sluggish, bottom-dwelling, nocturnal shark. Shallow to deep water, central California to Gulf of California.

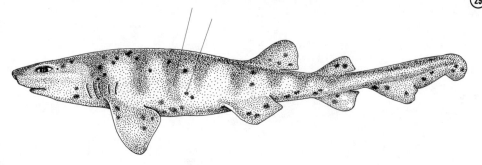

Swell Shark (*Cephaloscyllium ventriosum*)
Normal adult size 90-110 cm (35-43 in).
Brown areas and dark brown spots across
back. Eats small fish, crabs, shrimp, and
worms. Oviparous. Lays chitinous eggs,
which hatch 7.5 to 10 months later. Pups
measure 14-15 cm (6 in). Common in 5-20
fathoms, but strays to 160 fathoms. Prefers
rocky, algae covered areas. A sluggish bottom dweller. When disturbed, this shark can
double its girth by swallowing water or air
as a defense. Common from Monterey south.

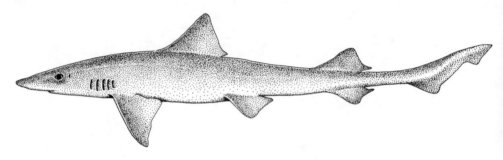

Gray Smoothhound (*Mustelus californicus*)
Adults are about 116 cm (46 in). Brown to dark gray above, white below. Spiracle behind eye. Albinism occurs in this species. Eats crabs, primarily. Feeds inshore, in shallow bays, sounds, rocky shores. Viviparous. Gestation 9-12 months. Litters of three to sixteen pups, measuring 20-30 cm (8-12 in), born in spring. Found down to 25 fathoms, but usually in three fathoms or less. Rare in northern California, more common in southern California and Mexico. Common in inshore waters of central California in the winter.

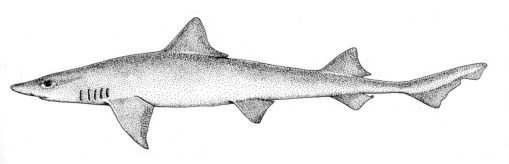

Brown Smoothhound, Sand Shark
(*Mustelus henlei*)

Adults range from 65 cm (26 in) to 97 cm (38 in). Bronze, reddish-brown above, white below. Has small teeth. Eats shrimp, worms, crabs, small fish, fish eggs. In turn, it is eaten by sea lions, sevengill sharks. Pups known to be eaten by large rockfish, other sharks. Viviparous. Six to twelve pups, measuring about 21 cm (8 in), born in open bays, away from marshes, in spring. Brown Smoothhounds travel in schools. Range is from Oregon to Peru, but most common in bays north of Monterey.

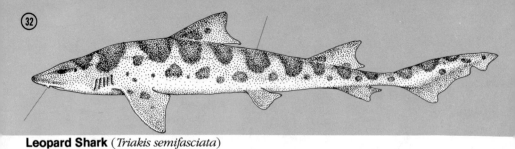

Leopard Shark (*Triakis semifasciata*)

Average size for males 150 cm (59 in), 180 cm (71 in) for females. Maximum 210 cm (83 in). Large sizes now rare in San Francisco Bay, which may indicate over-fishing. Leopard sharks are a popular sport species, easily recognized by their whitish-to-light-gray bodies with large black bars and dots, which increase in number with age. Albinism occurs. Leopard often burrows with its face into sand and mud in pursuit of echiuroid worms, ghost shrimp, blue mud shrimp, clam siphons. Also eats small fish, fish eggs, octopus, crabs and tunicates. Often feeds intertidally. In bays, leopard travels in size-segregated schools. Often rests on bottom. Females are mature at about 110 cm (43 in). Ovoviviparous. Gestation 9-12 months. Litter size to 34 pups. Young, measuring 18-20 cm (7-8 in), are born March to May, in or near marsh channels of Humboldt, Tomales, San Francisco Bays, Elkhorn Slough and similar sites south. Pups nearly double their size in their first year. Pups are endangered by commercial shrimp harvesting in south San Francisco Bay. A timid, harmless, inshore shark that ranges from Oregon to Gulf of California.

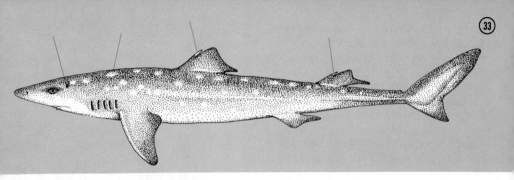

Spiny Dogfish (*Squalus acanthias*)

Adults 75-130 cm (30-51 in). Slate gray to brownish gray with small white spots and deep green eyes. Sharp spine in front of each dorsal fin. Albinism known. An opportunistic feeder that eats fish, fish eggs, shrimp, crabs and octopus. Males mature at 80-100 cm (31-39 in), or 11 years of age. Females mature at 100-124 cm (39-49 in) or 18-20 years of age. Ovoviviparous. Gestation of 22-24 months is one of the longest next to that of elephants. Pups are 20-30 cm (8-12 in) long two to eleven per litter. Before birth, they turn inside mother to emerge head-first, avoiding spine damage to her vent. Spiny dogfish travels in schools of hundreds, sometimes thousands. Damages commercial fishing nets, bait. In England, dogfish is used in fish-and-chips. Its liver oil was once an important source of vitamin A. Found to 400 fathoms. In north Atlantic and Pacific. On our coast from Bering Sea to Baja California.

Pacific Angel Shark (*Squantina californica*)
Average size 100 cm (39 in). May reach 155 cm (61 in). Sandy-gray to reddish-brown, with dark spots. Characterized by flat body, wide, toothy mouth, expanded pectoral fins. Eats fish. Ovoviviparous. Reproductive biology not well known. Nocturnal. By day, found buried in sand, mud or near rocks, ledges. Anyone handling this shark must be wary of bite. From southern Alaska to Baja California.

Pacific Electric Ray (*Torpedo californica*)
Length 91-137 cm (36-54 in). Blue-gray to brownish-gray with many dark spots. Head not distinguishable. Eats crabs, shrimp, worms, other invertebrates, fish. Ovoviviparous. Powerful electric current can stun prey and human handlers. Parasitic Cooper's Nutmeg Snail anesthetizes local area of resting ray, to penetrate and feed on ray's body fluids, without being shocked. Found buried in sand, mud, down to 150 fathoms. British Columbia to Baja California. **CAUTION: DO NOT HANDLE**.

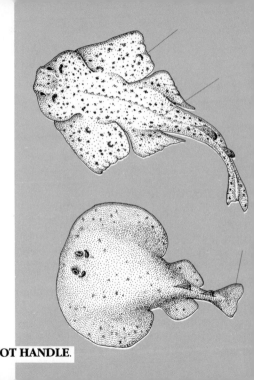

Thornback Ray (*Platyrhinoidis triseriata*)
Length to 91 cm (36 in). Brown, gray-brown, or olive-brown over back. Key features are two large dorsal fins and three rows of large, hooked spines on back and tail. Eats sand dwelling crabs, shrimp, worms, clams. Buries itself in fine sand and mud. Found down to 25 fathoms. From Monterey to Baja California. Rare north of Monterey.

Bat Ray (*Myliobatis californica*)
To 182 cm (72 in) wide. Dark brown, olive, blackish-brown. Key features are raised, massive head, single spine at base of whip-like tail. Slimy, no scales. Mouth has plate-like teeth used in crushing clams. Bat ray also eats echiuroid worms, shrimp, crabs, oysters, bay mussels, snails. Exposes clams by flapping wings, displacing mud, leaving large pot holes behind. Ovoviviparous. Gestation about 12 months. Ten or fewer young, about 22 cm (9 in) wide, born in summer. Often in large schools. Oregon to Gulf of California.

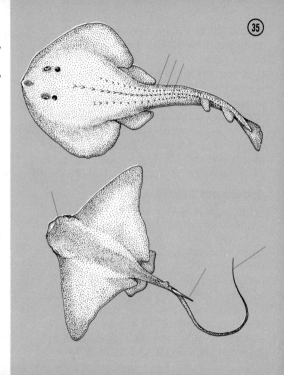

Round Stingray (*Urolophus halleri*)
To 56 cm (22 in) long. Brownish or gray-brown with yellow spots or reticulations. Uses large spine, midway on tail, in defense against predators like sharks. Eats clams, shrimp, crabs, small fish. Ovoviviparous. Large numbers of adults congregate off beaches to mate and give birth. One to six young born inshore in late summer. Found on sandy, muddy bottoms, also in bays and sloughs. To 12 fathoms. Eureka to Panama. **CAUTION: Stings when stepped on.**

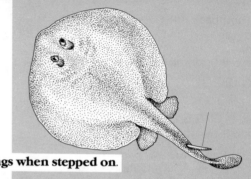

Shovelnose Guitarfish (*Rhinobatos productu*
Females 168 cm (5.5 ft), males smaller. Sandy-brown above. Long, pointed snout and single row of spines on back are characteristic. Eats crabs, shrimp, worms, clams, small fishes. Ovoviviparous. Up to 28 young per litter, born measuring about 15 cm (6 in) long. Often on bottom; covers itself with sand and mud. Nomadic, gregarious, often abundant. Lives in shallow coastal water down to 8.5 fathoms. In bays, sloughs, estuaries. San Francisco Bay to Gulf of California.

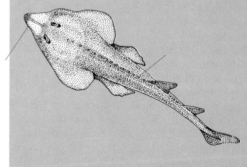

Big Skate (*Raja binoculata*)
To 183 cm (6 ft), some to 244 cm (8 ft). Gray,
brown, reddish-brown, or blackish, with
concentric zones of white spots around dark
eyespot on each wing. Eats crabs, shrimp
and bottomfish. Oviparous. Eggs up to 30 cm
long with several embryos per egg case.
Common at moderate depths to 60 fathoms,
Bering Sea to Pt. Conception; rare south to
Baja California.

California Skate (*Raja inornata*)
To 76 cm (30 in). Olive-brown, sometimes
with dark mottling and dark eyespots. Eats
crabs, shrimp, clams, bottom fish. Oviparous.
Eggs have long horns, one embryo per egg
case. Common inshore and in bays. Occasionally in deep water, to 366 fathoms.
Straits of Juan de Fuca to Baja California.

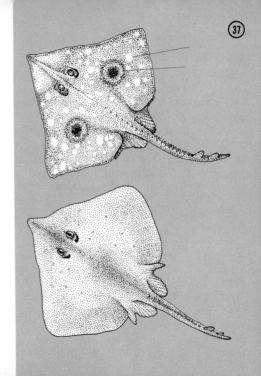

Starry Skate (*Raja stellulata*)
To 76 cm (30 in). Brown, gray-brown, often with light spots; has two eyespots with yellow centers and brown rings. This is our spiniest skate—much of its upper surface is covered with prickles. Eats crabs, shrimp, clams, fish. Oviparous. Eggs have lines; one embryo per egg case. In north, born June-July. Found on sand-mud bottom to 400 fathoms, Bering Sea to Baja California.

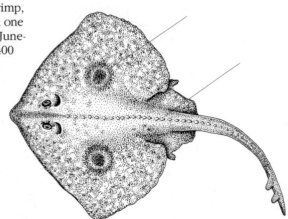

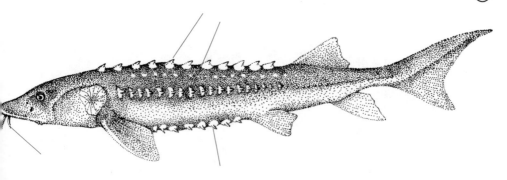

Green Sturgeon (*Acipenser medirostris*)

To 213 cm (84 in). Grayish-white to olive-green. Key features are bony plates on back and along sides, concave snout, and long barbels. Has a skeleton that is mostly cartilage, like that of sharks, but sturgeon is a primitive bony fish. Eats clams, shrimp, crabs, and worms in bays and estuaries by slurping them out of mud with protrusile mouth. Moves into fresh water to spawn, where it eats crayfish, snails, insect larvae. Taste buds are outside of mouth. Large females lay two to five million eggs, which hatch in two weeks to three months. Bering Sea to Ensenada.

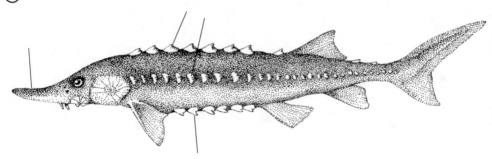

White Sturgeon (*Acipenser transmontanus*)

To 609 cm (240 in). May exceed 1,500 lbs. — largest North American freshwater fish. Gray, light below. Has more bony plates along sides, and barbels closer to snout tip, than green sturgeon. Spends most, if not all, of its time in freshwater. Moves upstream in winter or spring, downstream in summer. Eats snails, clams, crayfish, spawned out Eulachon (fish). Lays millions of eggs, in spring or summer. Young eat amphipods, mysid shrimp. Matures after 11 years. Gulf of Alaska to Ensenada.

Salmon Biology

Salmon and steelhead trout migrate from salt to fresh water to spawn. Such fish are called **anadromous**. The young leave fresh water to spend from one to four years in the ocean, some migrating thousands of miles out to sea. When mature, they use stars, moon, currents, electric and magnetic fields and their sense of smell as navigational aids in relocating the mouth of their home stream, which they enter to spawn.

Once in fresh water, the sense of smell becomes their primary guide in their journey upstream to shallow spawning areas. Males undergo tremendous physical changes in color and shape prior to spawning. After they reach the spawning area, females excavate gravel nests with their tails, displacing pebbles and silt. Males quickly fertilize the eggs, while females move upstream a meter or so to excavate another nest. The displaced gravel often washes downstream to bury the previously laid eggs. To hatch successfully, the eggs must be surrounded by pebbles and oxygenated water. Silt destroys eggs and newly hatched fish.

Young salmon and steelhead quickly become imprinted with the specific odor of their home stream. This will guide them back to the same stream as adults. Mortality is high from egg to adult. Dams, diversions, erosion, and silt are major problems that have reduced or eliminated salmon and steelhead in many rivers and streams.

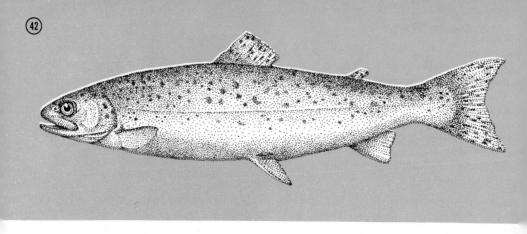

Steelhead Trout (*Salmo gairdnerii*)
To 114 cm (45 in), and 40 lbs. In the sea, bluish above, silver below with black spots on back and fins. Often a pink to red stripe on side. Mouth white. Greenish and less silver in fresh water. A steelhead is a rainbow trout that migrates to sea. Eats various crustaceans and fish. Adult spawns in stream gravel fall and winter. Young live in fresh water up to four years, then at sea for two to three years. Adults survive spawning. Bering Sea to San Luis Obispo County.

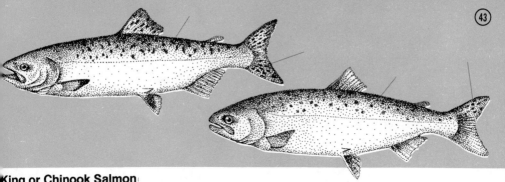

King or Chinook Salmon
(*Oncorhynchus tshawytscha*)

To 147 cm (58 in). Normally under 50 lbs. Some to 100 lbs. Greenish-blue to gray or black above with irregular black spots. Gums black at base of teeth. Eats various crustaceans, fish. Spawning runs occur in fall and in spring. Most young go to sea soon after hatching, but some may remain in stream. May range 1,000 miles out into Pacific. Most return to stream of birth in four or five years, others return later. Bering Sea to San Diego.

Silver or Coho Salmon
(*Oncorhynchus kisutch*)

To 98 cm (38 in), 31 lbs. Metallic blue back with black spots, silvery below. Gums white at base of teeth. Eats various organisms including fish, squid, crustaceans. Spawns in fall, early winter, then dies. Young stay in fresh water for one year, then move downstream into ocean. Mature in two to four years. Alaska to Baja California, but rare south of Santa Cruz.

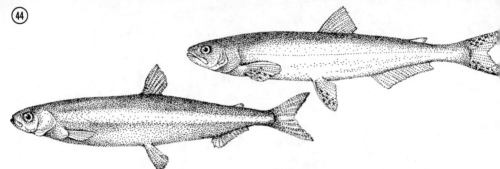

Surf Smelt (*Hypomesus pretiosus*)
To 25 cm (10 in). Olive-green or brown above, silvery below with bright metallic side stripe. Eats various small crustaceans, sometimes larval fish. Spawns throughout year in surf, on beaches, during the day. Females lay up to 30,000 eggs. Summer eggs hatch in 10-11 days, winter eggs take longer. A shallow water species. An important food for salmon, other inshore predators. Gulf of Alaska to Long Beach.

Eulachon (*Thaleichthys pacificus*)
To 25 cm (10 in). Bluish-brown above, silvery with fine black speckles below. Our only smelt with lines on gill covers. Juveniles and adults eat euphausiids (shrimp-like krill) and copepods. In north, adults move into rivers to spawn March-May. Most die afterward, some survive. Young are carried to sea by currents. An important inshore food for predators. Sometimes called "candlefish" because North Coast native Americans used dried fish as candles. Bering Sea to Monterey.

Plainfin Midshipman
(*Porichthys notatus*)

To 38 cm (15 in). From light to dark brown, olive or iridescent purple above, with yellowish belly. Several rows of silver-white spots (photophores) on sides, belly, and jaw are probably used in courtship. Scaleless. Feeds at night on fish, crustaceans. Buries itself in sand/mud during day. Male scoops depression out under rock for nest (often in intertidal zone). Female fastens up to 800 eggs on overhead rock. Male survives without food, often out of water at low tide, to guard nest 16-20 days before eggs hatch. Uses gas bladder to make grunting, groaning sounds. Called "singing fish." From Sitka to Gulf of California.

California Lizardfish
(*Synodus lucioceps*)

To 64 cm (25 in). Brown above, lighter below, with yellowish pelvic fin. Teeth large. Eats fish. Sits on bottom, propped up on pectoral fins to wait for small fish to come within range. Young are transparent. Found on mud, sand bottom, to 25 fathoms, but some to 125 fathoms. San Francisco to Guaymas.

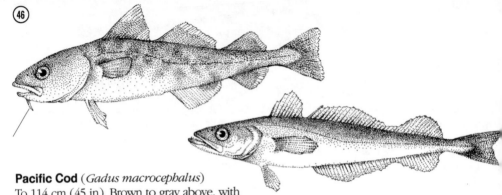

Pacific Cod (*Gadus macrocephalus*)
To 114 cm (45 in). Brown to gray above, with spots or lighter areas on back and sides. Some fins white-edged. Has chin barbel. Eats worms, crabs, mollusks, shrimp, fish. Spawns in winter. Eggs sink, are slightly sticky. Hatch in eight to thirty days, depending on temperature. Females mature at 40 cm, three years. A 60 cm female can produce over a million eggs. A bottom species, to 300 fathoms. Bering Sea to northern California, some found farther south.

Pacific Hake (*Merluccius productus*)
To 91 cm (36 in). Silver-gray with black speckles on back. Mouth black, large. Feeds mostly at night, on shrimp, sole, eulachon, tomcod, anchovy, smelt, other fish. Eaten by spiny dogfish and other predators. Spawns January to June. Eggs pelagic, float, hatch in three days or so. Adults found mid-water to near bottom. Most to 125 fathoms, some to 500. In schools. Alaska to Gulf of California.

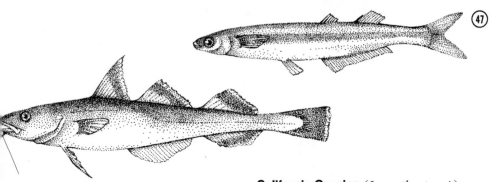

Pacific Tomcod (*Microgadus proximus*)
To 30 cm (12 in). Olive-green above, creamy-white below, with dusky fin tips. Small chin barbel. Dorsal fins spineless. Eats shrimp, probably other crustaceans. Little known about life history. Adults are found down to 125 fathoms, young shallower, often near surface. Over sand, mud bottom. Forms schools. A major food for large predators. Along coast, in bays. Bering Sea to central California.

California Grunion (*Leuresthes tennis*)
To 19 cm (7.5 in). Greenish above, metallic bluish side stripe, silver below. Eats small crustaceans. Spawns at night on sandy beaches, at high tide, from March-September, two to six nights after full and new moons. Female wriggles backwards into sand, leaving head out, to deposit eggs in sand. Eggs hatch 15 days later. Female may spawn several times per season. An inshore fish, found down to 10 fathoms. Forms schools. San Francisco Bay to Baja California.

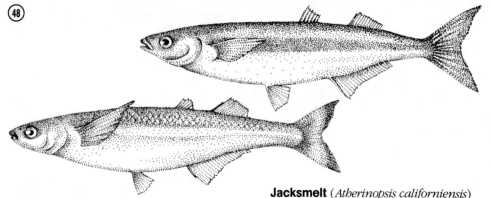

Topsmelt (*Atherinops affinis*)
To 37 cm (14.5 in). Green-blue above, metallic side stripe, silvery below. Teeth small, forked. Eats small crustaceans. Forms schools in March-April near entrances to bays. Spawns over shallow mudflats May-July. Eggs sticky, adhere to eelgrass, kelp. Females grow faster than males. Found inshore, at surface. British Columbia to Gulf of California.

Jacksmelt (*Atherinopsis californiensis*)
To 44 cm (17 in). Greenish-blue above, with silver side stripe, silvery-white below. Teeth not forked. Eats small crustaceans. Spawns in bays, estuaries. Eggs are sticky, forming massive grape-like clusters, adhering to algae, eelgrass, anchor line, etc., and are eaten by spiny dogfish, smoothhound sharks, others. Jacksmelt is an important food for larger predators. Forms schools. Oregon to Baja California.

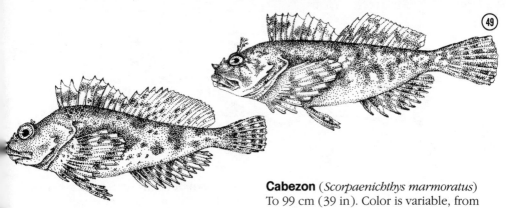

Red Irish Lord (*Hemilepidotus hemilepidotus*)
To 51 cm (20 in). Rarely over 30 cm. Reddish,
with brown, white, and black mottling.
Normally with four dark saddles on back,
white belly. Adult eats crabs, barnacles,
mussels. Female lays masses of tough pink
eggs on rocks, in spring, in intertidal or
subtidal waters. Kamchatka to Monterey.
Uncommon in California, where Brown Irish
Lord is more common.

Cabezon (*Scorpaenichthys marmoratus*)
To 99 cm (39 in). Color is variable, from
reddish olive-green, to brown, with mottling.
No visible scales. Body bulky. Eats fish,
crabs, abalone. Well camouflaged. Rests on
bottom in crevices, on top of rocks. Spawns
January-March (British Columbia). Greenish
eggs adhere to rock surface, are poisonous to
humans, perhaps to other animals. A 72 cm
(28 in) female is about 13 years old. Found
around rocky reefs down to 42 fathoms. Sitka
to Baja California.

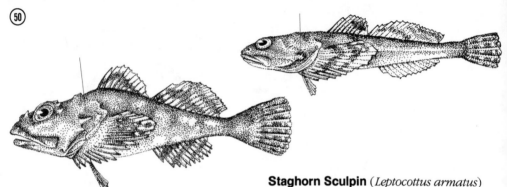

Great Sculpin

(*Myoxocephalus polyacanthocephalus*)
To 76 cm (30 in). Back is deep olive color with
four dark saddles. Brown bars on fins. Long,
straight, smooth preopercular spine. Eats small
fish, crabs and other invertebrates. Little
known about life history. Common on shallow
reefs. Bering Sea to Washington.

Staghorn Sculpin (*Leptocottus armatus*)
To 46 cm (18 in). Tan, greenish-brown, or
grayish-brown, with yellow-white belly.
Scaleless. Has large preopercular, antler-like
spines which project outward as defense
when fish is disturbed. A voracious feeder, it
eats small fish, shrimp, crabs, other invertebrates, and in turn, is eaten by striped bass,
sharks, cormorants. Spawns in winter.
Common inshore over sand, mud, especially
in bays, estuaries, lower reaches of coast
streams. Bering Sea to Baja California.

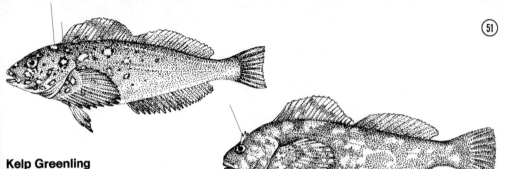

Kelp Greenling

(*Hexagrammos decagrammus*)
To 53 cm (21 in). Female has brown-gray body freckled with small reddish-brown to golden spots. Male, gray to brownish-olive body with irregular blue spots. Fins yellow-orange, mouth yellowish. Kelp greenling eats small fish, shrimp, decorator crabs, octopus and worms. Spawns October-November. Female lays large masses of pale blue eggs; male guards nest. Young eaten by steelhead, salmon. Found in rocky inshore areas, on the bottom. Aleutian Islands to southern California, but rare in south.

Rock Greenling

(*Hexagrammos lagocephalus*)
To 61 cm (24 in). Greenish to brown with dark mottling. Mouth bluish. Two red lines radiate back and down from eye. Males have large red blotches on sides. Rock greenling eats worms, shrimp, crabs, small fish. Reproduction similar to kelp greenling. Common in shallow rocky areas, exposed coasts. Bering Sea to Point Conception.

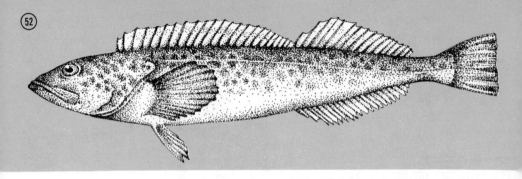

Lingcod (*Ophiodon elongatus*)
To 152 cm (60 in), some to 70 lbs. Mottled gray, brown, green, or bluish. Large mouth and canine-like teeth. Small scales. Lingcod is an aggressive, voracious predator, eating mostly other fish. Moves into shallow water in fall or early winter to spawn. Male guards nest of eggs attached to rocks. Young are found on sand or mud bottom in bays and inshore areas, adults down to 233 fathoms. From Kodiak Island to northern Baja California.

Rockfish Biology

Rockfish or rockcod are a common, diversified, and popular group, with over 60 species along the Pacific coast. They have large mouths, bright colors, choice flesh and large erectable dorsal spines that cause painful wounds to careless handlers. Their dorsal, anal and pelvic fin spines lack venom glands, but the slimy material around the spines can cause prolonged irritation and pain in puncture wounds.

Rockfish are major predators. While some species feed on macroplankton, such as euphausiid shrimp and hyperiid amphipods, others eat fish, various crabs, worms, shrimp and even small shark pups.

The reproductive cycle is quick. Eggs develop in about one month after internal fertilization. The large females of some species may contain up to two million eggs. The eggs hatch into tiny larvae (3-5 mm long) as they contact sea water. Rockfish larvae are pelagic, plankton eaters. When they reach 50 mm length, most move inshore and stay close to or on hard substrates, from tidepools to 17 fathoms. Some adults live to over 300 fathoms. Color changes with growth.

Rockfish are highly territorial and will defend their space against other rockfish intruders. They are often found in close proximity to each other indicating territories may be both small and seasonal. Rockfish also have strong attachment to a home-site. One study showed that yellowtail rockfish, tagged and removed up to 14 miles, returned to their exact home-site. Most stay close to their home-site areas. No migration has been observed for inshore species. When caught and suddenly brought to the surface, reduced external pressure greatly expands the swimbladder and makes the eyes bulge and stomach protrude from the mouth.

Copper Rockfish (*Sebastes caurinus*)
To 56 cm (22 in). Color is highly variable: orange-brown, olive, dull yellow, copper, or reddish. Posterior section of lateral line usually whitish or pink with white blotches. Two copper-orange bars usually angle down from eyes toward gills or pectoral fins. Eats other fish, crabs, shrimp. Found over rocky bottom down to 100 fathoms. Alaska to central Baja California.

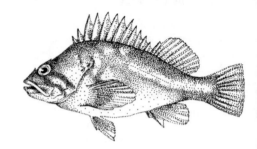

Calico Rockfish (*Sebastes dallii*)
To 25 cm (10 in). Broad, oblique bars on sides with irregular brown blotches. Overall color is yellowish-green, with brown to red brown streaks and spots on caudal fin. Eats fish and crustaceans. Found on or over sand or mud bottom down to 140 fathoms. From San Francisco to central Baja California, but rare north of Santa Barbara.

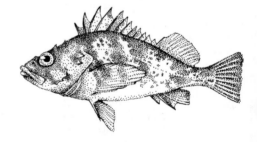

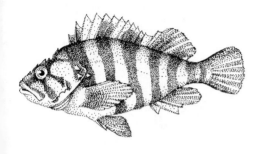

Treefish (*Sebastes serriceps*)
To 41 cm (16 in). Adults have five to six thick, black bars on an olive-yellow body, red-pink lips. Young have a more yellow body, lips not pink-red. Found around shallow rock reefs with caves and crevices to 25 fathoms. Solitary and highly territorial. San Francisco to central Baja California, but rare north of Santa Barbara.

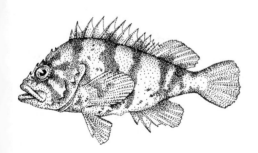

Tiger Rockfish (*Sebastes nigrocinctus*)
To 61 cm (24 in). Pink to red body has five black or dark red bars, four bars radiating from eyes. Adult sometimes has spots between bars. Anal and pelvic fins black-tipped in young. Found on rocky reefs, to 150 fathoms. Solitary. Very aggressive in defending territory. Alaska to central California.

Flag Rockfish (*Sebastes rubrivinctus*)
To 51 cm (20 in). Pinkish or pure white, with
broad red or reddish-black bars. First red
bar angles down from first dorsal spine across
gill cover. Found on rocky reefs and over
sand bottom, down to 100 fathoms. From San
Francisco to Baja California. Closely resembles redbanded rockfish.

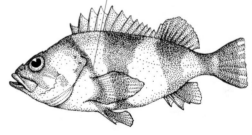

Redbanded Rockfish (*Sebastes babcocki*)
To 64 cm (25 in). Pinkish-white, with four
broad red or reddish-black bars. First red
bar starts in front of dorsal fin, touches upper
edge of gill cover and ends on the pectoral
fin. Young born April-May. Half of males are
mature at 38 cm, females at 42 cm (British
Columbia). Found over sand bottom, to 50
fathoms in north and 260 fathoms in south.
Aleutian Islands to San Diego, but uncommon
south of San Francisco.

China Rockfish (*Sebastes nebulosus*)
To 43 cm (17 in). Black to blue-black, mottled with yellow-white spots. A broad yellow stripe runs from third or fourth spine of dorsal fin down to and along lateral line to tail. Some blue around face, fins. Pronounced head spines. Eats crabs, shrimp, brittle stars, small fish. Solitary, found mostly in or near rock crevices or caves, to 70 fathoms. Alaska to San Miguel Island.

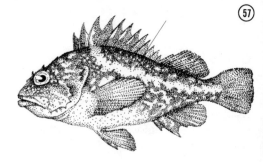

Black and Yellow Rockfish (*Sebastes chrysomelas*)
To 39 cm (15 in). Black to olive-brown with large irregular yellow blotches, spots. Yellow on third and seventh dorsal fin spines. Found close to rocks, crevices, caves, intertidal zone to 20 fathoms. Eureka to Baja California.

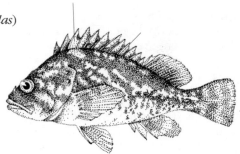

Gopher Rockfish (*Sebastes carnatus*)
To 39 cm (15 in). Brown to olive, mottled with pink to whitish blotches and spots. Lower lip yellow-orange. Eats crabs, squid, small fish. Found in shallow rocky areas and down to 30 fathoms. Eureka to Baja California. Closely resembles black and yellow Rockfish.

Brown Rockfish (*Sebastes auriculatus*)
To 55 cm (21 in). Light brown with dark brown mottling, dark brown blotch at top of gill cover. Belly pinkish. Females 31 cm long can produce about 52,000 young. Born in June (Puget Sound area). Widely distributed in shallow water, in bays, near shore, also to 70 fathoms offshore. Most common rockfish in San Francisco Bay. Alaska to Baja California.

Grass Rockfish (*Sebastes rastrelliger*)
To 56 cm (22 in). Dark green to olive color, mottled with light green, gray on sides. Lower pectoral fin rays pinkish in some adults. Thick body. Common in rocky areas, along jetties, in kelp, and eelgrass. Usually found in less than nine fathoms, but occasionally to 25 fathoms. Oregon to Baja California.

Kelp Rockfish (*Sebastes atrovirens*)
To 42 cm (16 in). Olive-brown to gray-brown with dark brown mottling. Belly sometimes pinkish. A solitary fish usually found off the bottom, suspended in mid water near kelp, or resting on it. To 25 fathoms. Sonoma County to central Baja California.

Green Spotted Rockfish
(*Sebastes chlorostictus*)
To 50 cm (19 in). Body yellowish pink with
many roundish bright green spots and
three to five large white to pink blotches on
back. Fins pink with yellow on membranes.
Found on sand or mud bottom, to 110 fathoms.
Copalis Head to central Baja California.
Greenblotched rockfish, *S. rosenblatti* has
green wavy lines in circles, but not in spots.

Quillback Rockfish (*Sebastes maliger*)
To 61 cm (24 in). Brown to blackish or
brown and light yellow with large mottled
orange areas, particularly about head, face,
and back. Membrane between dorsal
spines deeply incised. Found around rocky
reefs, caves, crevices. A common, solitary,
inshore rockfish in north. In south, found
down to 150 fathoms. Gulf of Alaska to
southern California.

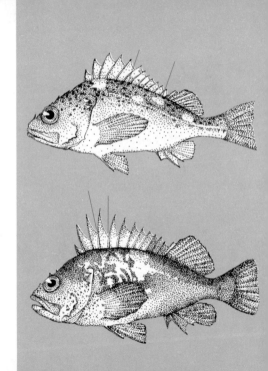

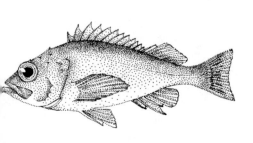 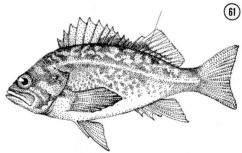

Stripetail Rockfish (*Sebastes saxicola*)
To 39 cm (15 in). Body pinkish-red to
yellowish pink with traces of green or
dusky saddles on back. Green stripes on
caudal fin sometimes faint. Young born 4 mm
long, in February (British Columbia).
Some mature at two years and 12.7 cm.
Half of the males are mature at 14.6 cm
(California). Females mature after reaching
17 cm, can release 15,000 young. Found
offshore on sand or mud bottom, to 230
fathoms. Common below 100 fathoms.
Southern Alaska to central Baja California.

Canary Rockfish (*Sebastes pinniger*)
To 76 cm (30 in). Orange, with gray blotches.
Lateral line usually in a clear gray area. Fins
bright orange. Head usually with three bright
orange stripes radiating from eye. Dark
blotch at end of spiny rays. Eats small fish,
krill. Young are born in January (British
Columbia). Half the population matures at
35.6 cm (14 in), five to six years old
(California). Females 48 cm carry about
260,000 young. Found over rocky bottoms
to 150 fathoms. Southern Alaska to northern
Baja California.

Vermilion Rockfish (*Sebastes miniatus*)
To 76 cm (30 in). Has reddish back mottled with gray, red-orange sides and belly, red fins, often with dark edges. Orange stripes radiate from eyes. Most of lateral line gray to white. Deep water specimens are more reddish, shallow water specimens more brownish overall. Found on shallow to deep rocky reefs. More abundant in shallow water, but found to 150 fathoms. Queen Charlotte Islands, to Baja California.

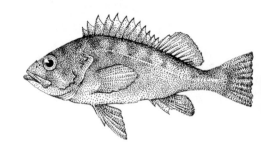

Bronzespotted Rockfish (*Sebastes gilli*)
To 71 cm (28 in). Reddish-orange with two bright, clear, orange areas below soft dorsal fin. Roundish bronze or brown spots on back and upper sides. Lateral line in a narrow red zone. Brown bars radiate from eyes. Upturned mouth. Common in deep water, southern California. To 205 fathoms. Monterey to northern Baja California.

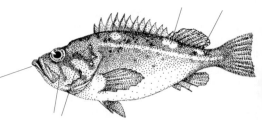

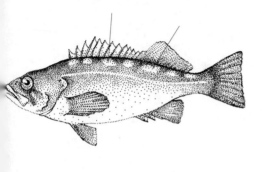

Olive Rockfish (*Sebastes serrandides*)
To 61 cm (24 in). Olive-brown above, pale below lateral line, with pale blotches along upper back, below dorsal fin. Fins olive, sometimes yellowish. Has nine rays in caudal fin. Eats mainly fish, squid, sometimes plankton. Found over rocky reefs and in clear, quiet kelp beds, usually above 17 fathoms, but occasionally to 80 fathoms. Northern California to central Baja California. Closely resembles yellowtail rockfish and kelp bass.

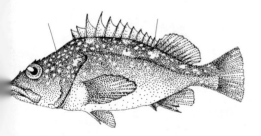

Starry Rockfish (*Sebastes constellatus*)
To 46 cm (18 in). Red-orange with three to five large white blotches on back and many small dots over body. Usually on deep rocky reefs, in caves and crevices. To 150 fathoms. San Francisco to southern Baja California.

Rosy Rockfish (*Sebastes rosaceus*)
To 36 cm (14 in), but rarely over 28 cm (11 in).
Red-purple mottling on back, often with
irregular patches of purple. Four to five white
blotches ringed by purple on back. One to
two purple bars radiating from eyes. Fins
orange-red, membranes greenish-yellow.
Found around caves, crevices on rocky reefs,
to 70 fathoms, but usually shallower. Puget
Sound to central Baja California, but rare
north of California.

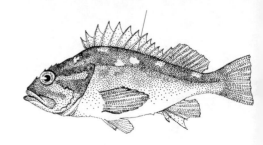

Blackgill Rockfish (*Sebastes melanostomus*)
To 61 cm (24 in). Dark red with black on rear
edge of gill cover. Inside of mouth is mostly
black. Fins red. A deep water species, found
to 420 fathoms, but young are found in
shallower water. Over sand or mud bottom,
Washington to central Baja California.

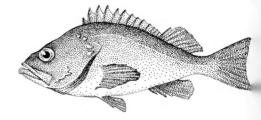

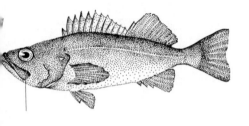

Bocaccio (*Sebastes paucispinis*)

To 91 cm (36 in). Olive-brown to red above; silvery-pink on sides. Young have brown spots on sides. Mouth large; lower jaw projects. Adults are voracious carnivores that eat mostly other fish, including rockfish. Lives to 30 years. Half are mature at 42 cm or four years (California). Females give birth in November; deliver a second brood in March. Young are 4-6 mm at birth. Wide-ranging. Adults are found over rocky reefs, sand or mud bottom, to 175 fathoms. Kodiak Island, Alaska to central Baja California.

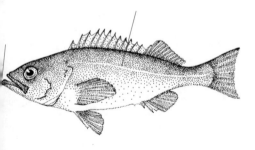

Chillipepper (*Sebastes goodei*)

To 56 cm (22 in). Mostly reddish-pink above, white below. White lateral line in a clear pink or red zone. Fins pink; soft dorsal and caudal fins dusky. Eats krill, small fish, squid. Half of males are mature at 29 cm. Found over deep rocky reefs and sand or mud bottom to 180 fathoms. Vancouver Island to southern Baja California.

Yelloweye Rockfish (*Sebastes ruberrimus*)
To 91 cm (36 in). Specimens up to 30 cm are orange to reddish with a white stripe along lateral line and onto head with a shorter second stripe below; black on pectoral, anal, and caudal fins. Larger specimens are more orange, lack lower stripe; lateral stripe may be pale. Eye bright yellow. Young born in June (Washington). Lives on rocky reefs, to 300 fathoms. Gulf of Alaska to northern Baja California.

Cowcod (*Sebastes levis*)
To 94 cm (37 in), 28 lbs. Mostly pinkish-red with four to five narrow, dusky, irregular vertical bars. Young have black spots near bars. In large specimens, the spine membranes of the dorsal fin are deeply notched. Eats fish, octopus, squid. Large females spawn over two million eggs or larvae, in winter or early spring. Adults are found on rocky bottom to 200 fathoms. Mendocino to Baja California.

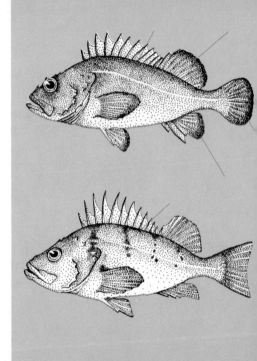

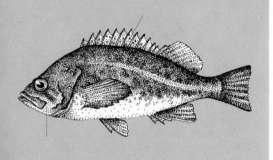

Black Rockfish (*Sebastes melanops*)
To 60 cm (24 in). Black or blue-black, mottled with gray. Some specimens have light patches on back, gray stripe along lateral line. Dark spots on dorsal fin. Upper jaw extends beneath and behind eye. Eats fish, squid, shrimp. Found on or over rocky bottom, sometimes over sand; from surface to 200 fathoms. Sometimes forms schools. Amchitka Island to San Miguel Island.

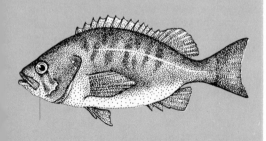

Blue Rockfish (*Sebastes mystinus*)
To 53 cm (21 in). Dark blue, mottled with light blue. No spots on dorsal fin. Upper jaw reaches eye, but does not extend past it. Young, gray with red streaks, black spots, are born in winter. They frequent offshore kelp beds in northern California, and are prey to ospreys (fish hawks). Blue rockfish eats large planktonic animals, jellyfish, salps, algae, small fish. Adults are usually found well above shallow or deep rocky reefs, in or near kelp beds, at surface to 300 fathoms. In schools. Bering Sea to Punta Banda.

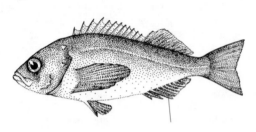

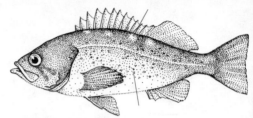

Widow Rockfish (*Sebastes entomelas*)
To 53 cm (21 in). Dusky, brassy-brown above, with some yellow, light below. Spiny dorsal fin light, other fins dark. Small specimens have faint orange streaks. Black membranes between rays of anal, pelvic, pectoral fins. Young eat plankton. Adults eat macroplankton, particularly hyperiid amphipods; sometimes small squid, anchovies. Half mature at four years, 32 cm. Widow rockfish forms large schools, mid-water, over rocky or sandy bottom. Found from surface to 200 fathoms. Kodiak Island to Baja California.

Yellowtail Rockfish (*Sebastes flavidus*)
To 66 cm (26 in). Olive, greenish-brown, or dark gray, with light areas, on back, and pale below. Red-orange-brown speckles on scales. Caudal fin dirty yellow; other fins may be yellow. Separated from look-alike olive rockfish by two yellow areas on gill cover, eight soft rays in caudal fin, and speckles on scales. Eats small hake, anchovies, lantern fishes, euphausiid shrimp, small squid. Young born January-February (Oregon). May live to 24 years. Yellowtail have a strong "homing" instinct. (See p. 53.) Mostly pelagic, over deep reefs, in schools, surface to 150 fathoms. Kodiak Island to southern California.

Surfperch Biology

Surfperches are one of the most commonly encountered inshore fish along our coast. Most are brightly colored with some silver, often barred or striped. Breeding males or females may be much more intense in color. Their bodies often seem laterally compressed, presenting a narrow form head on. Most species propel themselves with downward thrusts of the pectoral fins in a slightly jerky, up and down motion.

Surperches eat a variety of large zooplankton, invertebrates and some algae. Special grinding teeth in the backs of their mouths allow some species to crush small mussel and clam shells to digest the flesh inside. Some species act as cleaner fish, picking parasites off other fish.

Fertilization is internal. Males use the thickened front part of the anal fin to inject sperm, but fertilization of eggs often occurs months after copulation. Surfperches are **vivaparous**. Young are born alive often at 30-40 mm, after a gestation period of about a year. Developing embryos inside the mother use their highly vascular fins to absorb nourishment and oxygen. Litters are usually less than ten, but large females may bear up to 60. Some males are sexually active right after birth. Females mature a year or so later. Lifespan can range from three years for shiner surfperch to over nine years for black surfperch.

Surfperches are found in surf, kelp beds, on rocky reefs, in bays, estuaries, near piers, jetties and in tidepools. There are 21 species of surfperch, all limited to the Northern Pacific Region. Along our coast, 18 are marine, one of which, the shiner surfperch, enters fresh water. Another surfperch, the tule perch is restricted to freshwater along our coast. Two species live off Japan and Korea.

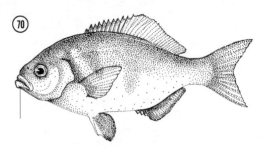

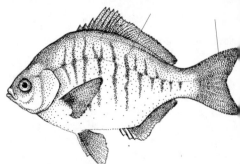

Rubberlip Surfperch,
Rubberlip Seaperch (*Rhacochilus toxotes*)
To 47 cm (18.5 in). Our largest surfperch. Silvery olive color fades to brassy-yellow below. Has thick white or pink lips. Pectoral fins yellow. First ray of soft dorsal fin shorter than third ray. Spiny rays shorter than soft rays of dorsal fin. Eats shrimp, amphipods, small crabs. Bears young in spring; 20 or more per female. Often in schools. Found in quiet waters of harbors, bays, around piers, kelp beds and outside the surf on open coast. Surface to 25 fathoms. Mendocino to Baja California.

Redtail Surfperch (*Amphistichus rhodoterus*)
To 41 cm (16 in). Body is silver-brassy with olive tinge along back, with eight to eleven reddish-brown bars on sides. All fins, especially caudal, red. Spiny rays of dorsal fin higher than soft rays. Redtail surfperch eats sand-dwelling crustaceans (mole crabs, amphipods) and mollusks, along steeply sloping sandy beaches. Found in surf, and down to four fathoms. Sometimes in bays, sloughs, backwaters. Vancouver Island to Monterey Bay. The most common surfperch caught in surf from central California north.

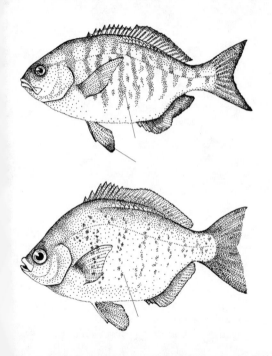

Barred Surfperch (*Amphistichus argenteus*)
To 43 cm (17 in). Silvery to brassy-olive color.
Back is marked with blue or gray. Has eight
to ten somewhat irregular brassy-gold bars on
side with spots in between. Eats mostly
sand crabs, also bean clams and small amphipods. Mates in fall or early winter. Specimens over 25 cm long usually have 45 or so
young born in March-July. Females grow
older and larger than males. Barred surfperch
is most abundant in surf along sandy, open
ocean beaches. Some found to 40 fathoms.
Bodega Bay to Baja California.

Calico Surfperch (*Amphistichus koelzi*)
To 30 cm (12 in). Silvery-blue to brassy or
olive. Sides have reddish to brownish bars
made up of small spots broken by lateral line.
Fins reddish; caudal fin dusky. Calico surfperch is common in surf of sandy beaches,
and to five fathoms. Cape Flattery to northern Baja California, but rare north of California.

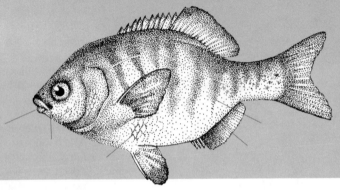

Black Surfperch, Blackperch, Butterlips
(*Embiotoca jacksoni*)

To 39 cm (15.5 in). Color varies, but overall is usually dark rusty-brown, with up to nine vertical bars on side. Lips orange to yellow-orange with a dark "moustache." Blue specks on scales and blue bar at base of anal fin. Has a noticeable patch of enlarged scales below pectoral fin. Eats worms, crustaceans, mollusks, small fish. Some black surfperch act as cleaners, picking parasites off other fish and their own kind. Found over rocky areas near kelp; sometimes over sand or mud bottom of bays, around piers or pilings. In San Francisco Bay, associated with oyster- or mussel-shell bottom with Gigartina kelp. Forms schools. Found at surface to 25 fathoms. Fort Bragg to Baja California.

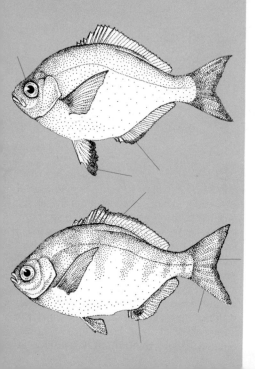

Walleye Surfperch
(*Hyperprosopon argenteum*)
To 30 cm (12 in). Body silver, often bluish above, sometimes with faint pinkish bars. Body highly compressed. Large eyes and striking black edge on pelvic fins are key features. Caudal and anal fins dark edged; breeding females have dark anal fins. Breeding males are darker overall. Eats small crustaceans. Breeds October-December. Five to twelve young born in spring. Found in surf, over sand or mud bottom, over rock reefs, kelp, around piers. Bays and outer coast to 10 fathoms. Vancouver Island to Baja California.

Silver Surfperch (*Hyperprosopon ellipticum*)
To 27 cm (10.5 in), but usually smaller. Silver-gray to greenish above, silver below; may have faint dusky bars on sides. Caudal fin pinkish. Anal fin usually with a black or orange spot. Dorsal and caudal fins may be dark edged. Found in surf, over sandy areas, around rocks and piers to 60 fathoms. British Columbia to northern Baja California.

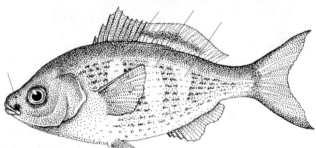

Shiner Surfperch, Shiner Perch
(*Cymatogaster aggregata*)

To 18 cm (7 in), but usually 10-13 cm (4-5 in). Silvery with rows of dark spots, forming stripes. (This feature is exaggerated in breeding males.) Stripes are crossed by three yellow bars, which are less noticeable in males in summer. A dark spot above corner of mouth is often present. Shiner surfperch eats zooplankton, small crustaceans, algae, mussels, barnacles. Sexes tend to be separate except during summer breeding season. Male courtship includes elaborate display involving fin nipping, darting back and forth appearing to isolate selected female. Sperm is stored in ovarian compartment five to six months before eggs fertilized. In spring, females move over intertidal mudflats in San Francisco Bay at high tide to bear up to 36 young per litter. Males are mature at birth. Females give birth in their second year. Found around eelgrass, piers, pilings of bays, sloughs, in calm areas of exposed coast. Enters fresh water of rivers. Usually in shallow water, but known to 80 fathoms. Forms loose schools. Southern Alaska to northern Baja California.

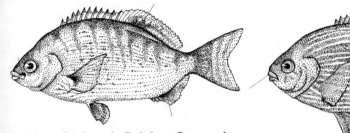

Rainbow Surfperch, Rainbow Seaperch
(*Hypsurus caryi*)

To 30 cm (12 in). Body has orange and blue horizontal stripes. Orange bars on back. Blue spots and streaks on head. Black spot near corner of upper lip. Pelvic fins bright orange with whitish-blue edge, but soft dorsal and anal fins have dark blotches. Belly flat but may turn upward in front of anal fin. Some rainbow surfperch act as cleaners, picking parasites off other fish. Found over rocky bottom, along edges of kelp beds, occasionally over sand, but not in surf. To 22 fathoms. Forms schools in the fall for breeding. Cape Mendocino to northern Baja California.

Striped Surfperch, Striped Seaperch
(*Embiotoca lateralis*)

To 38 cm (15 in). Body has 15 or so horizontal reddish-orange and blue stripes below lateral line. Stripes are curved above lateral line. Blue spots and streaks on head and operculum. Upper lip often black. Pelvic fins dusky. Eats small crustaceans, worms, mussels, herring eggs. Up to 44 young per litter are born in June or July (British Columbia). Found over reefs, in kelp beds, bays, around piers. Offshore to 12 fathoms. Southern Alaska to Baja California.

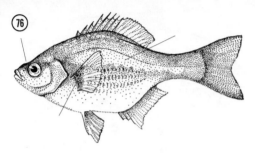

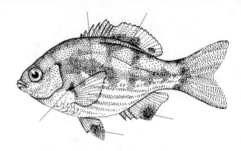

Kelp Surfperch (*Brachyistius frenatus*)
To 22 cm (8.5 in). Brassy to golden-brown: dark above, sometimes with blue spots or streaks; paler and often reddish below. Fins plain, sometimes rosy. Black specks on upper pectoral. Sharp upturned snout and oblique mouth. Short dorsal fin with large space to caudal. Kelp surfperch eats seaweed isopods, other kelp-associated crustaceans. Picks parasites from other fish. Forms schools in summer for breeding. Matures in first year (California). Rarely found far from kelp. At surface to 15 fathoms. Southern British Columbia to central Baja California.

Dwarf Surfperch, Dwarfperch
(*Micrometrus minimus*)
Less than 7.6 cm (3 in). Silver-blue, greenish to olive on back; yellow, green-silver below, with a large, irregular dark stripe on side, crossed by dark bars. Black triangle at base of pectoral fin. Dorsal, anal, pelvic fins with black blotches. Dwarf surfperch eats algae, small invertebrates. In rocky inshore areas; around seaweed, tidepools. To five fathoms. Bodega Bay to central Baja California.

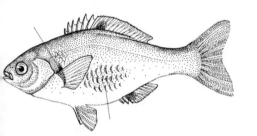

Reef Surfperch, Reefperch
(*Micrometrus aurora*)
To 18 cm (7 in). Blue-greenish above, fading to silver below, often with orange-gold stripe from pectoral to near caudal fin. Scales between anal and pectoral fins are black-edged. Black triangular blotch at base of pectoral. Eats algae, small invertebrates. Found in shallow rocky areas, tidepools, to 3.3 fathoms. Tomales Bay to north central Baja California.

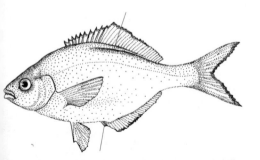

White Surfperch, White Seaperch
(*Phanerodon furcatus*)
To 32 cm (12.5 in.) Body is silver, bluish to olive above, silver below and may have yellowish to rosy tint. Fins yellowish, with black line at base of dorsal fin, sometimes a black spot on front edge of anal fin. White surfperch are usually found near piers, in bays, sandy areas, quiet water and offshore rocks to 23 fathoms. Vancouver Island to northern Baja California.

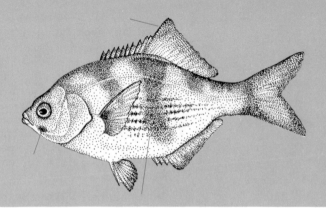

Pile Surfperch, Pileperch
(*Damalichthys vacca*)

To 44 cm (17.5 in). Blackish-gray to brownish above, silvery below, usually with a broad vertical dark bar at mid-side. Often a dark spot below eye. Breeding males quite dark. Caudal fin deeply forked. Soft rays taller than spiny rays. Pile Surfperch eats various mussels, small clams, barnacles, shrimp. Mates in late summer or fall; fertilization of eggs delayed until December-February. Young born mostly July-August, with up to 61 per litter (Oregon). Found on rocky shores, kelp beds, pilings; common in bays, estuaries. To 40 fathoms. Southern Alaska to north central Baja California.

riped Bass (*Morone saxatilis*)

122 cm (48 in), 90 lbs. Greenish-black. Sil-
r sides with six to nine black stripes on
ale rows; white belly. Anadromous, moving
gularly between fresh and salt water. Lives
ostly in or near estuaries. Adults eat various
h, including young "stripers." Larvae feed
plankton, copepods, mysid shrimp. Adults
ove into fresh water in fall, stay until
ring when they spawn at the surface in
en river water. After spawning, adults
turn to San Francisco Bay or the ocean.
ales mature at two to three years, females
five to six years.

riped bass are native to east coast. Over 430
ripers were introduced in San Francisco
Bay and delta in 1879 and 1882. By 1899,
stripers had dispersed to below Mexican
border, up to British Columbia. Largest population was in San Francisco Bay. This popular sport fish has been steadily declining
since the 1960's, because of one or more
of the following: adult population is so low
that egg production is also low; plankton
food supply of young is greatly reduced due
to diversions of delta water for agriculture
in southern California; millions of young fish
are removed from delta by Central Valley
water diversions; and population is stressed
by toxic chemicals released into prime
habitat.

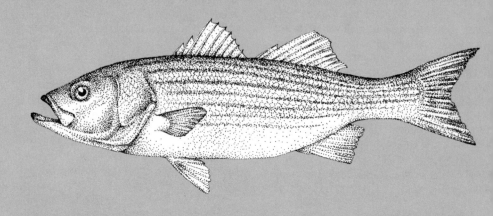

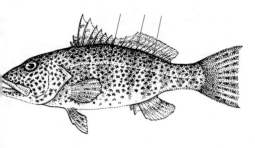

Spotted Sand Bass
(*Paralabrax maculatofasciatus*)
To 56 cm (22 in). Olive-brown above, pale below, with round black spots on fins and body, broad faint bars on back. Young have dark stripes. Spotted sand bass eats crabs, shrimp, fish. On sand or mud bottom, near rocks, in eelgrass, to 33 fathoms. Monterey to Mazatlan.

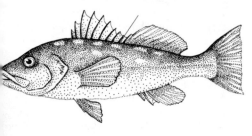

Kelp Bass (*Paralabrax clathratus*)
To 72 cm (28.5 in). Olive-brown above, cream below, with pale blotches on back, yellowish tinge on fins. Breeding males have orange chin and lower jaw. Kelp bass eats crabs, shrimp, squid, octopus, worms and fish. Spawns from late spring to fall. A slow-growing fish, occurs around reefs, wrecks, kelp beds, to 25 fathoms. From mouth of Columbia River to Bahia Magdalena, but most abundant in southern California.

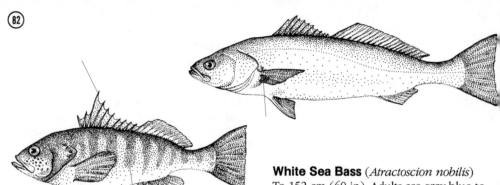

Barred Sand Bass (*Paralabrax nebulifer*)
To 65 cm (25.5 in). Gray, greenish-brown
above, with dark bars on side, pale below;
with gold-brown, orange spots on head. Third
dorsal spine is long. Eats crabs, shrimp, fish.
Usually found over sand bottom, sometimes
near or among rocks, to 100 fathoms. Santa
Cruz to southern Baja California.

White Sea Bass (*Atractoscion nobilis*)
To 152 cm (60 in). Adults are gray-blue to
copper above, white-silver below, with dark
spots and black spot at base of pectoral.
Young, to 61 cm, have three to six dusky
bars on sides, and yellowish fins. White sea
bass eats fish, squid. Congregates inshore
April-August to spawn. All mature at 75 cm.
Found in schools over rocky bottom, or in
kelp beds, to 67 fathoms. Juneau to southern
Baja California. Rare north of California.
This species is a croaker and *not* related to
preceding basses.

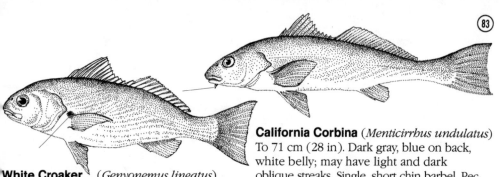

White Croaker (*Genyonemus lineatus*)
To 41 cm (16 in), usually less than 30 cm.
Silver-brassy above with dark specks, pale
below with a hint of wavy lines along scale
rows. Caudal fin dark-edged, other fins
yellow-white. Has small black spot at top of
pectoral fin base. Produces croaking noise
with swim bladder. Eats various bottom invertebrates. Matures at 13-15 cm. Spawns
November-May. Forms schools. Most are
found inshore, to 17 fathoms, but some to
100 fathoms. British Columbia to southern
Baja California. Rare north of California.

California Corbina (*Menticirrhus undulatus*)
To 71 cm (28 in). Dark gray, blue on back,
white belly; may have light and dark
oblique streaks. Single, short chin barbel. Pectoral fin black. Swim bladder absent, cannot
make sounds like other croakers. Adults eat
sand crabs, small shrimp, bean clams,
worms. Spawning occurs offshore June-
September, mostly in July-August. Usually
found in small groups, but large fish are
solitary. Some migrate 50 miles. Almost
always over sand or mud bottom on open
coast or in bays, sloughs. To eight fathoms.
Commonly caught by surf and pier fishermen
in southern California. Point Conception to
Gulf of California.

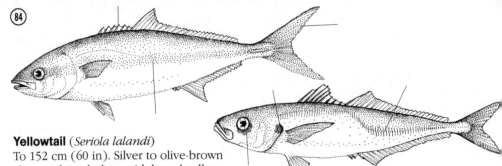

Yellowtail (*Seriola lalandi*)
To 152 cm (60 in). Silver to olive-brown above, silvery below, with broad yellow stripe head to tail. Fins, particularly caudal, yellow. Eats anchovies, sardines, mackerel, squid, pelagic red crabs. Acts as a cleaner fish, picking parasites off blue sharks. Many spawn at two years old, nearly all at three years, June-October, but July-August are peak months. Most spawn off central and southern Baja California. Found around offshore banks and islands, kelp beds, rocky areas, to 38 fathoms, but at surface in summer. Forms schools. British Columbia to Chile.

Jack Mackerel (*Trachurus symmetricus*)
To 81 cm (32 in). Metallic blue-olive-green, sometimes mottled above, silver below. Dark under eye, dark spot on gill cover. Lateral line dips sharply behind pectoral fin. Caudal fin has yellow-red tones. Eats mainly microplankton, but also lanternfish, saury, squid. Most are mature at three years, 31 cm. Spawn February-May in middle of night. Eggs near surface. Fish pelagic, at surface to 100 fathoms, in large schools. Southern Alaska to southern Baja California.

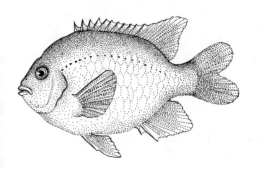

Garibaldi (*Hypsypops rubicundus*)
To 36 cm (14 in). Adult is solid bright orange, with green eyes. Young Garibaldi is red-orange or brick-red with iridescent blue spots/blotches. Eats mostly attached invertebrates. Propels itself with pectoral fins. Spawns March-July. Male clears sheltered rock of all growth prior to spawning. Female deposits eggs, male fertilizes them and stubbornly guards nest against intruders. Adult defends home territory and, when disturbed, produces thumping sounds. Found over reefs, in kelp beds, to 16 fathoms. Monterey to southern Baja California, but rare north of Point Conception. **CAUTION: This fish is protected by law from all forms of collecting. PLEASE RELEASE UNHARMED**.

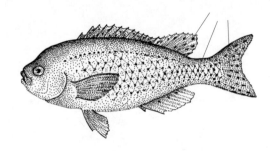

Blacksmith (*Chromis punctipinnis*)
To 30 cm (12 in), usually smaller. Gray-blue
with black spots on rear part of body, soft
dorsal, and caudal fins. Young are purple in
front, yellow at rear. Young pick parasites
off other fish. Spawns in summer. Male cleans
nest site, herds female to it, then guards
eggs until they hatch. Found on reefs, kelp
beds, to 45 fathoms. Monterey to central
Baja California, but rare north of Point
Conception.

California Barracuda, Pacific Barracuda (*Sphyraena argentea*)

To 122 cm (48 in). Brown-blue above, silver below. Caudal fin yellow. Some have oblique bars on back. Has strong jaws and large teeth. Eats mostly other fish. Most are mature at two years. Spawns in summer. Female may spawn several times per season. Eggs are pelagic. A schooling species that lives inshore to ten fathoms. Migrates north in summer, south in autumn. Although highly esteemed for edible flesh, some are occasionally toxic. Kodiak Island to southern Baja California, but rare north of Morro Bay.

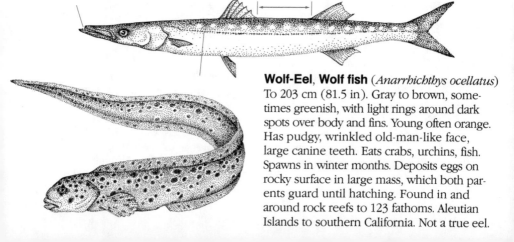

Wolf-Eel, Wolf fish (*Anarrhichthys ocellatus*)

To 203 cm (81.5 in). Gray to brown, sometimes greenish, with light rings around dark spots over body and fins. Young often orange. Has pudgy, wrinkled old-man-like face, large canine teeth. Eats crabs, urchins, fish. Spawns in winter months. Deposits eggs on rocky surface in large mass, which both parents guard until hatching. Found in and around rock reefs to 123 fathoms. Aleutian Islands to southern California. Not a true eel.

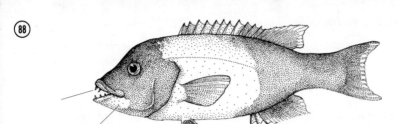

California Sheephead
(*Semicossyphus pulcher*)

To 91 cm (36 in). Male has black head, red eye, red, pink or dusky-red mid body, blackish rear. Female is solid rose, red-brown. Both sexes have white chins. Young are red-orange with white side stripe. Large black blotch on most fins. Older male may have large bump on head. Large teeth protrude from mouth. Sheephead eats urchins, scallops, lobsters, crabs, abalone. All are female until they reach 30 cm, then change into males. Spawn in spring or summer. Eggs are free floating. Adults may live 50 years. Found on rock reefs, in kelp forests, to 48 fathoms. Monterey to Cabo San Lucas.

Senorita (*Oxyjulus californica*)

To 25 cm (10 in). Dusky yellow overall; often orange-brown above, pale below. Caudal fin has large black area. Eats small snails, crabs, isopods, worms, larval fish. May pick parasites off other fish. Spawns May-August. Matures at one year. Often buries itself in sand at night to sleep with head protruding. Found on rocky reefs, in kelp beds, to 55 fathoms. Salt Point, Sonoma County to Cedros Island.

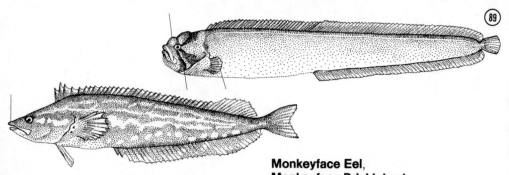

Giant Kelpfish (*Heterostichus rostratus*)
To 61 cm (24 in). Usually yellow-brown to green and purple with light mottling, sometimes with silver stripes or irregular bars. Color pattern matches surrounding algae. Hard for divers to see. Eats small crustaceans, mollusks, and fishes. Giant kelpfish is usually found resting on or among kelp blades, among algae covered rocks, in eel grass, to 22 fathoms. British Columbia to Cabo San Lucas.

**Monkeyface Eel,
Monkeyface Prickleback**
(*Cebidichthys violaceus*)
To 76 cm (30 in). Usually solid olive, gray or black with two dark streaks radiating down from eye. May have orange spots on body, orange edges on fins. Adult has lumpy ridge top of head. No pelvic fins. Eats crabs, shrimps, isopods, algae. Lays eggs on rocks, guards them until hatching. Found inshore in crevices of rocky areas, tidepools, to 13 fathoms. Southern Oregon to north central Baja California.

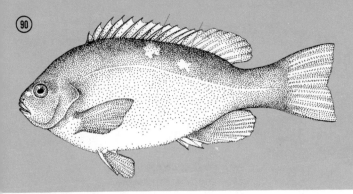

Opaleye (*Girella nigricans*)
To 66 cm (27 in). Olive-green, gray-green with two light spots on back. Large specimens may not show these spots. May have a white bar across head between eyes. Eats seaweed, eelgrass. One theory suggests it gets its nourishment from the invertebrates on the algae. Spawns April-June. Reaches maturity in two to three years. Found on shallow reefs, kelp beds, to 16 fathoms. San Francisco to Cabo San Lucas.

Tuna Biology

Pacific mackerel, skipjack, bonito, albacore, yellowfin and bluefin tuna are closely related members of the mackerel family, known collectively as tunas. They occur in tropical, temperate, and cold seas, and often make long migrations. One tagged albacore migrated 4900 miles in 11 months.

Tunas tend to be nearly scaleless, heavily-muscled, torpedo-shaped, and fast. Their dorsal fins can fold into grooves, to minimize water resistance and facilitate both escape and the pursuit. They lead roving, predaceous lives far offshore in deep, clear open ocean, usually hunting near the surface, but also at great depths.

Most fish have temperatures close to that of the surrounding water, because they lose body heat through the gills. But tunas can be up to 18 degrees warmer than the sea. They retain body heat by means of a counter-current heat exchange system which allows muscle tissue to operate more effectively. As a result, they can swim faster, and can extend their forays farther north into colder water.

Tunas generally spawn in open ocean. Females lay thousands of millimeter-sized eggs, each buoyed by a globule of oil.

Schools of tunas may have over 50,000 individuals. They often feed beneath dolphins. The dolphins attract tuna fishermen who capture the tunas in big, bag-like purse seines. The process also traps, and drowns, the air-breathing dolphins, often significantly reducing their numbers. There has also been a substantial worldwide decline in some tuna species, particularly bluefins. Progress is being made to reduce the number of dolphins killed in tuna fishing, but strong conservation measures and improved fishing techniques are needed to save both tunas and dolphins from extermination.

Skipjack, **Skipjack Tuna** (*Euthynnus pelamis*)
To 102 cm (40 in). Dark, slightly metallic-blue above, silver below, with four to six horizontal dark bands. Eats other schooling fish. Males mature at 39 cm; females at 34 cm. In tropical water, spawning may occur year around. Highly migratory, traveling in large schools, inshore to offshore. World-wide, nearly all oceans. Here, British Columbia to Peru.

Pacific Mackerel,
Chub Mackerel (*Scomber japonicus*)
To 64 cm (25 in). Dark green to blue-black above with many wavy streaks passing just below lateral line. Lower sides silvery with dark blotches. Dorsal fins widely separated. Eats schooling fish (anchovies, herring) and squid. Spawns near shore, April-July, possibly more than once per year, each time producing several hundred thousand pelagic eggs which hatch in three days. Many mature in second year. A highly migratory, schooling fish. Found at surface to 25 fathoms. Gulf of Alaska to Chile.

Pacific Bonito (*Sarda chiliensis*)

To 102 cm (40 in). Greenish-blue above, silver below with oblique stripes on back. Eats sardines, anchovies, pelagic fish, squid. Spawns from January-May (southern California). Inshore and pelagic, in schools. Alaska to southern Baja California, but rare north of California. A more southern population is found off Peru.

Albacore (*Thunnus alalunga*)

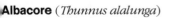

To 137 cm (54 in), and 76 lbs. Dark blue above, silver-white below. First dorsal fin deep yellow. Second dorsal, anal fins light yellow. Has extremely long pectoral fin. Eats pilchards, herring, anchovies, saury, small rockfish, squid, euphasiid shrimp, near the surface. In turn, is eaten by striped marlin, others. Spawns January-June, southwest of Hawaii. Migrates to mid-Pacific, sometimes Japan, in winter; returns to California coast in summer. Can move six miles per day, but, aided by upwelling currents off Oregon coast, may cover 15 miles. Seems to prefer clear offshore water. Usually in large schools. Worldwide. Southern Alaska to southern Baja California.

Yellowfin Tuna (*Thunnus albacares*)
To 193 cm (75.6 in), and 125 lbs. in our area.
Dark blue above, silver-gray below. Some
have yellow side stripe. Fins yellowish. Young
have white bars and spots on belly. An
aggressive, fast-swimming predator, which
eats various schooling fishes. Forms large
schools. Found offshore, in open ocean, at
surface to 138 fathoms. Atlantic, Pacific,
Indian Oceans. On our coast, from Point Conception to Chile.

Bluefin Tuna (*Thunnus thynnus*)
To 188 cm (78 in), but some known to 304
cm (120 in). Most in our area weigh 10-45
lbs. Largest known weighed over 1,490 lbs.
Dark blue-black on back, silver below. Belly
has white spots and lines. First dorsal fin is
blue and yellow; second dorsal red-brown.
Has short pectoral fin. A speedy, voracious
predator. Eats squid and schooling fish
(anchovy, jack mackerel, sardine), and is
occasionally eaten by sperm whales. Some
from our coast migrate to Japan. Found
inshore and offshore, worldwide. In our
area, from Shelikof Strait to south of Baja
California.

wordfish (*Xiphias gladius*)

457 cm (180 in) and 1200 lbs. Black,
rownish-black above, light-brown below.
dult lacks scales, pelvic fins, and teeth on
ws. A speedy predator that feeds on vari-
us fish, squid, pelagic crustaceans. May use
word" to stun or kill prey. During whal-
g era, swords of this fish and billfish were
ften found broken off
the wooden hulls
f ships, sometimes causing leaks. Found
shore and offshore, surface to 33 fathoms.
ligratory. Usually solitary. Worldwide. On our
ast, Oregon to Chile.

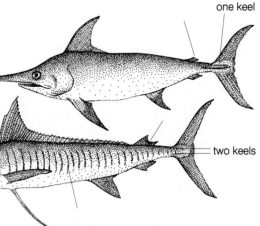

one keel

two keels

triped Marlin (*Tetrapturus audax*)

408 cm (160 in). Dark blue above, silver-
hite below. Sides have 15-25 blue bars or
ertical rows of spots. Jaws have teeth. Adult
as pelvic fins and scales. Eats fish, squid,
elagic crabs and shrimp. Spawns May-August
northern Pacific. Found at surface to mid
depths, offshore, but common around oce-
anic islands. Pacific and Indian Oceans.
Cape Mendocino to Chile; but more prevalent
south of Point Conception.

Halibut, flounder, sole, turbot, sanddabs and tonguefish are generally known as flatfish. Of 600 flatfish species, most are marine. They range in size from tiny sanddabs 15 cm (6 in) long to Atlantic halibut over 300 cm (10 ft) long and 700 pounds.

Flatfish have both eyes on one side of the head. They lack swimbladders. They rest the eyeless side on the bottom, where their flat form offers minimal resistance to strong currents and allows them easily to maintain position. They often bury themselves in the sand or mud with rhythmic fin movements, leaving only eyes and mouth exposed. Many can change color to match surroundings.

When flatfish spawn, females release their eggs into open water. Eggs of some species have oil droplets which make them float. Other species' eggs lack oil and sink. Eggs may hatch in seven or more days, depending on temperature. At first, flatfish larvae look like most fish with one eye on each side of the head. Within about 24 days after hatching, one eye begins to migrate to the opposite side of the head. Species in which the left eye moves to the right side of the head are called **right-eyed**, and vice-versa. Most species are strictly one or the other. A few species have both right- or left-eyed individuals. The location of mouth and gill cover will help you determine whether they are right or left. Once eye migration is complete, the young fish settle to the bottom blind-side down. Flatfish are extremely important to us as food. Unfortunately, some Pacific halibut have been found with higher than acceptable levels of methyl mercury in their flesh.

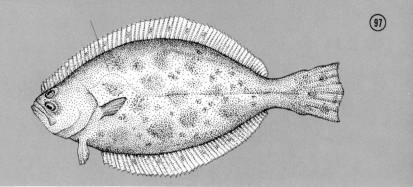

California Halibut (*Paralichthys californicus*) o 152 cm (60 in). Uniform dark brown-lack, often mottled light/dark. Key features re large mouth, sharp teeth, and lateral line rched over pectoral fin. Usually left-eyed, ome with eyes on right. Eats anchovies, ueenfish, squid. Often feeds off the bot-om, but may leap out of water in pursuit of urface schools of anchovies. Eaten by ngel sharks, electric rays, sea lions, dolphins. Spawns in shallow water, February-July. Male matures at two to three years, females at four to five years. Found on sand bottom inshore to 100 fathoms. Tagging studies show that this species does not move far from settling site, some to 140 miles maximum. Common near entrances to many harbors, bays, estuaries. Northern Washington to southern Baja California.

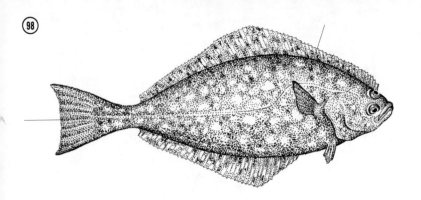

Pacific Halibut (*Hippoglossus stenolepis*)
To 267 cm (105 in) and 500 lbs, but a few to 800 lbs. Our largest flatfish. Dark brown-blackish with spots, mottling. Almost always right-eyed. Jaw does not extend past middle of eye, as it does in California halibut. Eats fish, crabs, clams, squid, other invertebrates. Spawns November-January at 150-225 fathoms. Large females can produce two to three million eggs. Larvae are concentrated mainly below 109 fathoms. When halibut is 18 mm long, eye on left side begins migration to right side. As larvae grow, they rise and drift inshore. They settle on bottom when six to seven months old, then move offshore at age of five to seven years. Found from surface to 600 fathoms, but usually above 225 fathoms. May migrate 1,000 miles, Bering Sea to northern Channel Islands.

Rock Sole (*Lepidopsetta bilineata*)
To 60 cm (23.5 in). Light to dark brown or
gray, sometimes mottled with red or yellow.
Lateral line arches abruptly over pectoral fin
with a short branch along back that ends
before arch. Adults eat clam siphons, brittle
stars, shrimps, worms, small fish. Females
lay to 1.3 million eggs, February to April.
Found on gravelly bottom, to 200 fathoms,
but usually at less than 100. Sea of Japan,
Bering Sea to Tanner Bank.

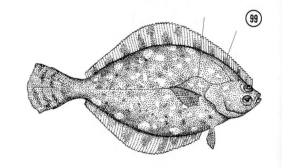

C-O Turbot, C-O Sole
(*Pleuronichthys coenosus*)
To 36 cm (14 in). Dark brown to blackish
with conspicuous dark spot at mid-body.
Caudal fin has dark spot preceded by backwards C-shaped bar. Long branch of lateral
line along back reaches mid body. Four to
six dorsal rays extend over to blind side.
Young are found inshore, adults offshore to
190 fathoms, over sandy-rocky bottom.
Southern Alaska to northern Baja California.

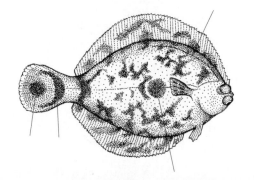

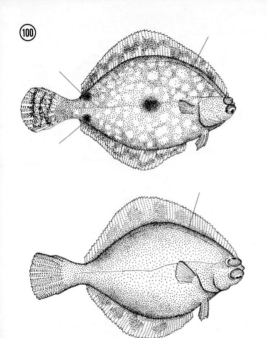

Spotted Turbot (*Pleuronichthys ritteri*)
To 29 cm (11.5 in). Brown, gray-brown with small light spots. One, or sometimes two or three, dark spots at back of dorsal fin and at mid body. First six rays of dorsal fin on blind side. Found inshore, to 25 fathoms. Morro Bay to southern Baja California.

Curlfin Turbot, **Curlfin Sole**
(*Pleuronichthys decurrens*)
To 37 cm (14.5 in). Brown, blackish, reddish-brown; mottled. Branch of lateral line passes along back past mid-body. Right-eyed. First nine to twelve dorsal rays are on blind side. Eggs are pelagic, hatch after seven days. Curlfin is found on sandy or muddy bottom, to 290 fathoms. Prince William Sound to north central Baja California.

Diamond Turbot (*Hypsopsetta guttulata*)
To 46 cm (18 in). Dark gray, greenish, often with bright blue-gray spots. Yellow on underside of mouth. Lateral-line branch along back more than half-way to caudal fin. Right-eyed. Found on mud, sand bottom to 25 fathoms. Cape Mendocino to Magdalena Bay.

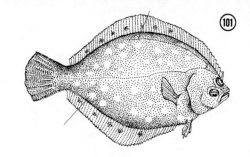

English Sole, **Lemon Sole** (*Parophrys vetulus*)
To 57 cm (22.5 in). Brown, occasionally spotted. Belly side white, pale yellow, tinted red. Upper eye visible from blind side. Eats clams, clam siphons, worms, shrimp, small crabs, brittle stars. Spawns January to March (British Columbia). Eggs pelagic, but sink several hours before hatching. Hatch in 90 plus hours, depending on temperature. Young are about 20 cm long at two years. Young are found in shallow water, but adults shift between shallows in spring and deeper water in winter. To 300 fathoms. Highly migratory, ranging 700 miles or more. Unimak Island to Baja California.

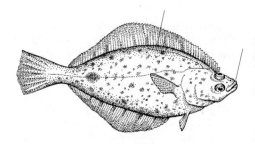

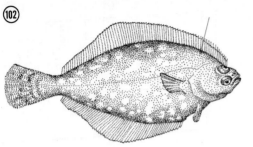 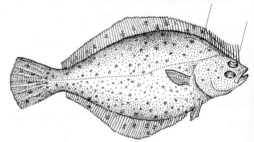

Butter Sole (*Isopsetta isolepis*)
To 55 cm (22 in), but usually less than 30 cm. Brown with dark and light mottling; sometimes lightly spotted in yellow or green. Yellow on edges of dorsal and anal fins. Lateral line has low arch over pectoral fin. Right eyed. Eats worms, shrimp, sand dollars, young herring. Spawns February-April. Lives 10-11 years (34-39 cm). Migrates to shallow water in summer, deep water in winter. Found to 200 fathoms but usually at lesser depth. Bering Sea to Ventura.

Sand Sole (*Psettichthys melanostichus*)
To 63 cm (25 in). Gray, brown or greenish with black speckles. Lateral line has low arch over pectoral, with short branch along back. First five to eight dorsal rays mostly free of membrane. Right eyed. Eats speckled sanddabs, herring, anchovies, crabs, shrimp, worms. Spawns January-July. Eggs hatch in about five days. Mostly found in shallow, inshore waters, but some to 100 fathoms. Bering Sea to Redondo Beach, southern California.

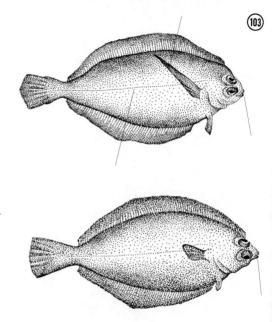

Rex Sole (*Glyptocephalus zachirus*)
To 59 cm (23 in). Light brown; fins dark-edged with long pectoral fin mostly black. Lateral line straight, unbranched. Small mouth. Right eyed. Biology not well known. Spawns in spring. Slow growing. Lives to 24 years. Found offshore to 350 fathoms, most abundant below 33 fathoms. Bering Sea to northern Baja California.

Dover Sole (*Microstomus pacificus*)
To 76 cm (30 in). Brown; fins dusky. Blind side light-dark gray, sometimes with red areas. Slimy, slippery. Right-eyed. Eats burrowing animals like worms, shrimp, clams (siphons). Spawns November-February (California). Eggs pelagic. Unlike other flatfish, eye migration and physical transformation is delayed for months. Females grow faster, live longer. North-south migration of 100-350 miles occurs. Found over mud bottom to 500 fathoms. Bering Sea to central Baja California.

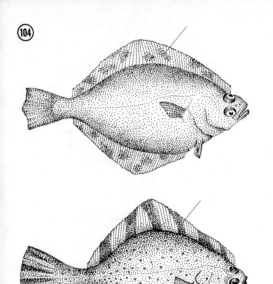

Petrale Sole (*Eopsetta jordani*)

To 70 cm (27 in). Brown. Dorsal, anal fins have faint blotches. Right eyed. Large mouth. Eats shrimp, sand lance, herring and various other bottom animals. Spawning occurs at 200 fathoms, in late winter or early spring (British Columbia). Female lives up to 25 years, male up to 19. Moves into deep water in winter, into shallow water rest of year. To 250 fathoms. Bering Sea to northern Baja California.

Starry Flounder (*Platichthys stellatus*)

To 63 cm (25 in). Brown to nearly black. Dorsal, anal, caudal fins have dark bars alternating with yellow-orange bars. Rough tubercles (modified scales) on body. Can be right- or left-eyed. Eats crabs, shrimp, worms, clams, small fish. Spawns in shallows, December-January (California, later in north). Found inshore in bays, estuaries, outer coast, to 150 fathoms. Japan, Bering Sea, to Santa Barbara.

Pacific Sanddab (*Citharichthys sordidus*)
To 41 cm (16 in). Light brown mottled with dark brown, sometimes with yellow-orange spots. Bony ridge above lower eye. Left eyed. Eats worms, small crustaceans, young anchovies. Spawns from February (Puget Sound) to summer (California). Some females may spawn twice. Half of females are mature at 19 cm long. Lives seven years. Found on soft bottom to 300 fathoms. Bering Sea to southern Baja California.

Speckled Sanddab (*Citharichthys stigmaeus*)
To 17 cm (7 in), but rarely over 13 cm. Brown, tan with speckles, spots. Ridge above lower eye absent. Left-eyed. Eats small crustaceans, worms. In turn, is eaten by sea birds, sea lions, seals, other fish. Spawns March-September. Found in inshore, shallow waters (50 fathoms), sometimes to 200 fathoms, on sand or mud bottom. Common in bays, estuaries. Southern Alaska to southern Baja California.

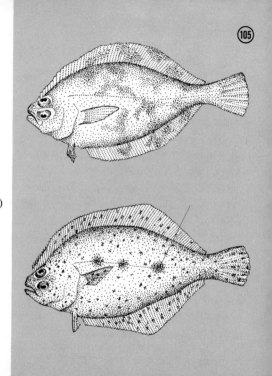

References

Boschung, Herbert T., Jr., James D. Williams, Daniel W. Gotshall, and David K. and Melba C. Caldwell. *The Audubon Society Field Guide to North American Fishes, Whales, and Dolphins.* Alfred A. Knopf, 1983

Budker, Paul. *The Life of Sharks.* Columbia University Press, 1971

Castro, Jose I. *The Sharks of North American Waters.* Texas A&M University Press, 1983

Dozier, Thomas A. *Fishes of Lakes, Rivers and Oceans.* Time-Life Films, Inc., 1978

Eschmeyer, William N., Earl S. Herald and Howard Hammann. *A Field Guide to Pacific Coast Fishes of North America.* Houghton Mifflin Company, 1983

Fitch, John E., and Robert J. Lavenberg. *Marine Food and Game Fishes of California.* University of California Press, 1971

Fitch, John E., and Robert J. Lavenberg. *Tidepool and Nearshore Fishes of California.* University of California Press, 1975

Gotshall, Daniel W. *Pacific Coast Inshore Fishes.* Sea Challengers Press, 1981

Hart, J.L. *Pacific Fishes of Canada.* Fisheries Research Board of Canada, 1975

Herald, Earl. *Fishes of North America.* Doubleday & Company, (no date listed)

Lineaweaver, Thomas H., III, and Richard H. Backus. *The Natural History of Sharks.* J.B. Lippincott Company, 1970

Marshall, N.S. *The Life of Fishes.* Universe Books, 1970

Miller, Daniel J. and Robert N. Lea. *Guide to the Coastal Marine Fishes of California.* Marine Resources Region, California Department of Fish and Game, 1972

Nikolsky, G.V. *The Ecology of Fishes.* T.F.H. Publications, 1978

Steel, Rodney. *Sharks of the World.* Facts on File, 1985

Whitehead, Peter. *How Fishes Live.* E.P. Dutton & Company, 1977